NOTICING

365 DAYS OF CALM REFLECTIONS

KARYN HENLEY

ANDON PRESS
NASHVILLE

Noticing: 365 Days of Calm Reflections

www.KarynHenley.com

ISBN 979-8-9870550-0-7 (pbk), 979-8-9870550-1-4 (epub)

INTRODUCTION

If you ever visit Cheekwood Botanical Gardens in Nashville, Tennessee, take a tour through the mansion. I used to be a docent there, and if you were on one of my tours, I would point out elements of the mansion worth noticing. One would be the view through the south windows. I would encourage you to notice a long, rectangular pool attended by two gray stone Greek goddesses: Thalia, muse of comedy, at one end and Urania, muse of astronomy, at the other. This is the "reflecting pool." When I first learned its name, I thought it came from the reflections in the water—sky, clouds, trees, statues, and you, if you're looking into it. But its name actually refers to the practice of reflecting. As in thinking. Considering. Pondering. *Musing.* That's why there are benches by the pool and probably why the statues of the *muses* stand there looking so thoughtful.

I've been reflecting on *reflection*. The word is related to *flex* and *flexible* and originated with the Latin word *reflectere*, which means "to bend back." Energy (like light, heat, and sound) bends back after hitting a surface and returns to us in what we experience as a *reflection*. In the sense of musing, reflection is our thoughts bending back to us. Noticing, then reflecting on what we notice can lead to reverence, awe, wonder, and gratitude. It can be a type of meditation, a kind of prayer, a sacred, holy practice. As such, it's wondrously important, because as the moon reflects the light of the sun, so we reflect to the world whatever we reflect on. My wish for you, as you join me in this year of readings, is that you will be gently drawn to notice and reflect on all that's beautiful, peaceful, wondrous, and hopeful and reflect that back into the world. Our world needs you.

Two notes:

First, since I live in the northern hemisphere, I've begun this book with winter. If you live in the southern hemisphere, you may want to start with the summer months.

Second, it may take you more than a year to get through these 365 readings. No pressure. You can skip some entries and even double back and start again. Use this book in whatever way suits you.

WINTER

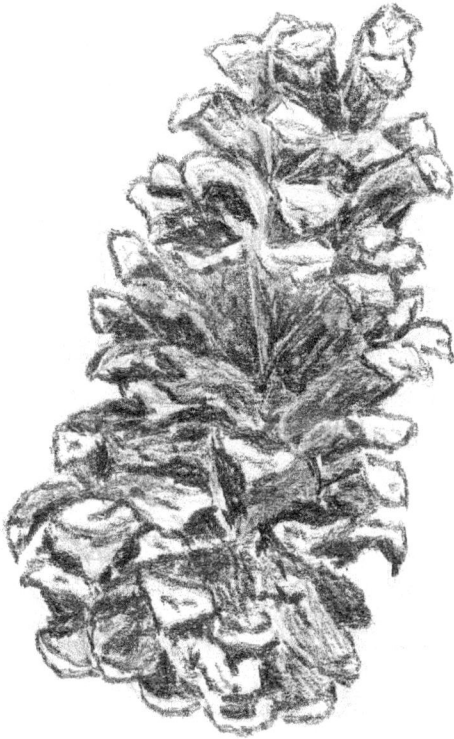

JANUARY

1

A new day, a new month, a new year. In my neighborhood, it has dawned bright and breezy with clouds scudding across the sky. The sun peeks in from the east now and then to splash down tree trunks and redden bare branches. I open my windows to a chorus of birds reveling in this amazingly mild weather. But it's too mild, I know. Mountains of blue-gray clouds are approaching from the southwest. In a little over 24 hours, temperatures are expected to drop, and we may have snow showers. Between now and then? Storms. Strong wind. Hail maybe. Possible tornadoes. These transition times between balmy and cold are wild. Dangerous even. But, oh, while the mild breeze blows through the windows, I have hopeful thoughts of spring.

2

It's mid-afternoon. Storms have blown through, and the sky is a soft gray. Raindrops drip from gutters and tap at windowpanes. The elm outside, which was thrashing about in the wind just an hour ago, is now steady and still, and a flock of birds—I can't see what kind—is perched in its upper branches. I count them.

Twenty, twenty-five, maybe thirty. As I'm counting, one darts away, one hops to a different branch. They are overseers of this rain-soaked yard, carolers on this chill day.

3

Two of my favorite things are windows and treetops. As I took my seat in the choir loft at church this morning, I looked across the balcony to see both. The tip-top branches of a tree were framed in one of the high windows against the backdrop of gray-blue clouds. The branches rocked back and forth in the wind like a painting that had come alive. Maybe it was dancing to our songs.

4

I've been brushing up on my drawing skills by reading a book I've had since college when I took art classes: *The Natural Way to Draw* by Kimon Nicolaides. He points out that even objects we think of as motionless have movement. So now I'm noticing the movement of all kinds of objects around me. The squat teapot, round and solid with its handle that arches up and over from its backside to descend to its spout, which flows up and out to offer itself. The two matching teacups, each circling up from their bases wider and wider to their rims. A vase that sits heavily on my counter, rounding at its belly then flaring up and out to hold carnations with wavy petals and a spider mum wildly splaying its petals this way and that. All of these are motionless, but even in their stillness, they hold movement.

5

The weather watchers I follow for up-to-the-minute forecasts are saying that in the falling temperatures today, the rain will change to sleet that will, in turn, become snow. It's a soup day. A hot chocolate day. A warm sweater, cat-in-the-lap day.

6

The snow dances
in a whirling frenzy,
swirling,
sweeping,
sliding.
Then the wind subsides,
and the flakes settle
to a slow drift
until the next gust
whips it up again,

and in a whirling frenzy,
the snow dances.

– kh –

7

Snow perches in dollops on branches and sits piled in thick mounds on the deck rail and stairs. Bits of grass peek through the lawn's white blanket, and the tips of daffodil leaves have emerged. My five-year-old grandson is playing in our snowed-in treehouse. He sails down the slide in a flurry of snow and calls, "Is this an excitement day?" "Yes," I call back. "It's an excitement day." And truly, it is.

8

I'm watching a lampshade gently sway in the updraft of warm air from a heating duct on the floor. Across the room, shamrocks bob in rising air from a matching duct below their flower pot. They are visual echoes of each other, quietly bobbing and swaying to the flow of warm air as if the shamrocks are acknowledging the movement of the lampshade, and the lampshade is respectfully nodding back. It's a subtle dance, and I wonder why I'm drawn to it. I wonder why I note it in my journal. Maybe it's the way these two things, so unalike, are moving quietly and gently in harmony. Maybe it's witnessing this backdrop of life that carries on whether I'm here to see it or not, the way breeze, trees, stars, and seasons play their role in the flow of life. Maybe it's because now that I've seen these two, I'm part of their dance.

9

René Descartes said of clouds, "If I can explain their nature, . . . one will easily believe that it is possible in some manner to find the causes of everything wonderful about Earth." Out of all the questions—who, what, when, where, how, what if— the one I gravitate to is why. Why do cardinals stick around during winter but lots of other birds fly south? Why do we often have ice storms instead of snow? For a long time, I tried to find answers for all of my whys. Then I read something Flannery O'Connor wrote. She said that we have a habit of trying to explain everything and have all the answers, which leaves no room for mystery. I'm still a why person. But I'm trying to feel comfortable in living with unanswered questions. More and more, I'm leaving room for mystery.

10

In the southeast corner of my back yard stands "my" elm tree. I often admire it from where I sit at my desk, looking out the window. This morning, its mid layer of branches—its second story if it were a house—crosses the sky at the exact place where the blue lower sky meets the upper sky, a layer of soft pink clouds lit by the rays of the rising sun. My elm looks like it's cradling the dawn.

11

The blooming garden that I wander through in this cold season is better known as the supermarket floral department. It's at the front of the grocery store I go to, and I always slow down to admire the blooms. Sometimes I buy a bouquet, usually a mix of flowers, usually what's on sale. Today, I bought a bright yellow spider mum for one vase and a soft salmon-pink carnation for another. I'm told that in Japan, a single mum petal placed in the bottom of a wine glass is said to bring a long and healthy life. My yellow spider mum has long, healthy-looking petals. Maybe I should skip the vases, pour myself a glass of wine, and test the theory.

12

I stretch and yawn watching the sun rise over hazy hilltops on the horizon. A dusky pink sky peeks through the lace of bare branches, growing rosier by the minute, turning the hills into a line of purplish humps outlined in glowing orange. As I watch, the sky softens into a wash of pink-gold across an edgeless expanse of clouds. Above this is a layer of misty, pink-gold, pillow-like clouds that eases up into a field of sleepy blue. A spot of sun, the center point of all this color, brightens in a break in the clouds, making the bamboo beside my house gleam and glitter. The bamboo leaves gently wave good morning as the sunlight stretches in this slow yawn of morning.

13

I woke up to an icy fringe of winter hanging halfway down the windows. Icicles had appeared overnight. As the morning sun finds them, they sparkle with such bright flares that I squint when I look directly at them. Even so, I lean closer to see the inner art of these icicles, waves and whorls that glitter from the inside. This art is temporary, of course. The icicles are beginning to drip. I step back from the two windows above my desk to get a wider view, which changes my perspective. My two windows look like

large eyes surveying my backyard world, and the
icicles look like bangs. This morning, my house is
wearing icy bangs.

14

Heavy rain is pounding us today, streaking the
windowpanes south and west, beating a constant tap-
pat on the roof. The bamboo is bowed and dripping.
Pine branches bob in the rush of water. Drops
pummel the deck, spraying out in tiny explosions. I
imagine trying to type as fast as this rain pelts down.
I'm fast, but I'm no match for this frantic unseen typist,
a ghost writer, racing to get stormy thoughts down
before the clouds move on.

15

Math is a wonder, the way the numerals are a code representing numbers, which are the actual amounts of things. I was never a math whiz, and I'm still slow at it, which is probably why I'm impressed with how numbers are so consistent and have such interesting connections. It amazes me that nine times any given number is one less than that given number plus whatever adds up to nine. Like 9 x 3 = 27 or 9 x 7 = 63. I wish I had known that long ago. It would have really helped me when we played Multiplication Baseball in third grade. I can see how math is a thing of beauty with lots more patterns than I know. But how could it not be beautiful? It's a part of nature.

16

Today I learned a new word that's really an old word: "flizzoms." It comes from nineteenth century English dialect and means "small flakes or particles in liquid." Like the bits of cereal left in the milk after you've eaten all the flakes. Or the tiny cracker crumbs in your soup after you've dipped crackers in it. So stay alert when you dunk a cookie in your coffee. You might find some flizzoms.

17

Great billows of smoke rise
from my backyard neighbor's chimney.
A gentle breeze plays with it,
pushes it east,
thins it.
When the breeze stills,
the smoke drifts straight up,
a gray-white cloud
that disperses into the air,
becoming
an invisible part of the breeze
that drifts
through the neighborhood,
nudges a dog-walker,
who raises her head
and takes a deep breath
at the scent of smoke
on this cold,
gentle-breeze
day.

– kh –

18

Today was sunny, but the temperature barely got up to the freezing point. I kept checking the thermometer until it reached 32 degrees—at 3:00 in the afternoon. Assuming this would be the warmest part of the day, I went out to the mailbox at the street to get the mail. I didn't linger at all, because I hadn't put on my coat, just a sweatshirt. On my way back to the house, I heard a lone chickadee calling, "Chick-a-dee-dee-dee, chick-a-dee-dee-dee." I wondered if he had found a warm spot and was happy about the sun. Or maybe he was singing to keep himself warm. Or maybe he was just saying hello to this human who was hurrying through his yard without a coat. Maybe he wanted me to sing too.

19

My grandmother used to make what she called "ranch toast." She would put thin squares of butter in four spots on the toast and then put it under the broiler until the butter melted, leaving the unbuttered parts a toasty brown. Ranch toast looked like a window with four yellow panes in a toasty brown frame. I always wondered why Grandmother didn't spread the butter all over the bread. Recently, as I was buttering a piece of toast, the answer dawned on me. Grandmother kept her sticks of butter in the refrigerator, so the butter was hard. She cut thin slices with a small, sharp knife. Each slice was a square, a "windowpane." Because the cold butter was too hard to spread without tearing the bread, she toasted it that way. I'm a grandmother now. My oldest grandson is off to college this year. And I just now figured out the secret of my own grandmother's ranch toast. Life is funny that way.

20

Part of a hinge on one of my kitchen cabinets broke with a loud pop. It's a part that keeps the cabinet door closed when you shut it. Over the years, I think every one of the cabinet hinges in our kitchen has lost this same part with this same popping sound. I roll my eyes when I hear the telltale pop. Not again, I think. (The part is made of plastic, which doesn't make much sense for something that gets a constant workout.) What an amazing thing a hinge is. I'm noticing hinges everywhere now. Big, heavy-duty ones on doors in my house and car. Smaller ones on my laptop. Tiny ones on a music box. And the hinges I constantly use as I move around: elbows, knees, fingers, wrists, ankles. Today I'm grateful for hinges.

21

The electric warmer in the birdbath
has kept it from freezing overnight.
The water steams in the frigid morning.
In the center of this pool
sits a domed spinner
the size of a large orange
with legs and a wire whisk
that spins around and around
making the water ripple and pulse
in rings of tiny waves,
sending them to the edge,
the birdbath's outer shore,
the rim of the oasis.
The ripples summon the birds:
"Psst!
Here's water.
Running water.
Not frozen solid
but fresh and clear."
In the cold,
robins flock in,
circle around the rim,
a meeting of the minds it seems,
perhaps discussing how spring
has been betrayed
by the ice-cold wind.
I imagine the oldest robin nodding wisely.

"Yes, yes, spring will come.
Not today.
Not tomorrow.
But drink up.
Spring will come."

– kh –

22

For a fun outlook on the year ahead, look at the way George Ellis, an English poet, described the months:

Snowy, Flowy, Blowy,
Showery, Flowery, Bowery,
Hoppy, Croppy, Droppy,
Breezy, Sneezy, Freezy.

23

The stars awaken a certain reverence,
because though always present,
they are inaccessible.

– Ralph Waldo Emerson –

My younger son has a star app on his phone. He can hold the phone up to any part of the sky, and the app will show what stars are there, even if they're not fully visible. It shows us all the stars we cannot see. Well, not all. Beyond those stars are more. And beyond those are even more. Nothing makes me feel as small as gazing up into the star-filled sky.

24

C.S. Lewis once wrote, "I am a product of long corridors, empty sunlit rooms, upstairs indoor silences, attics explored in solitude, distant noises of gurgling cisterns and pipes, and the noise of wind under the tiles. Also, of endless books." His sensory description carries such a feeling of wonder and gratitude that it struck me as an invitation to complete the thought in my own way. I'm a product of Kool-Ade tea parties shared with cousins sitting around the rim of an old tractor tire. I'm a product of waiting for my mom to pick me up or for my little sisters to finish with lessons or appointments. I'm a product of the hum of evaporative coolers, the scent of gardenias, the search for snails in the dirt, and the ever-present Texas wind, hot and dry in the summer, frigid and cutting in winter. I'm a product of bold, expansive sunsets, new interstate highways, only three channels of television, and books. What sensory world are you a product of?

25

"Skyscapes more than landscapes remind us that you don't need to rush across the world to be surprised. Just step outside and pay attention to the everyday stuff that most people miss." – Gavin Pretor-Pinney, *A Cloud a Day*

Most moments in life offer us the gift of wonder. We just need to notice them. Sometimes it's the wonders right in front of us that surprise us most.

26

There are only two ways to live your life.
One is as though nothing is a miracle.
The other is as though everything is a miracle.

– Albert Einstein –

My garden is now a collection of dried arrangements, mostly in shades of brown but in fascinating shapes. Brittle stems lean this way and that, some with dark seed heads on top, others—like the hydrangea—with faded, dry petals that have kept their shape. As I look closer, the garden reveals its treasures: translucent petals marbled with empty brown veins, pincushion seed heads that have dropped most of their seeds, dainty skeletons of leaves. All this stands before a backdrop of evergreens—stately pines and arbor vitae, a magnificent magnolia, prickly mahonia. The bare garden is not really bare at all.

27

Clouds now and again
Give a soul some respite from
Moon-gazing—behold.

– Matsuo Basho, translated by Einbond –

We have a half-moon tonight, climbing the bare branches of our trees. As it rises and pulls free, filmy clouds brush past it, a veil of magic gracing the night-world. This is the same moon that Matsuo Basho gazed at almost 400 years ago. In the 1600s, he wrote, "Behold." In the 2000s, I do.

28

In my old drawing book, the artist Kimon Nicolaides writes, "Loosen up. Relax . . . There are many things in life that you cannot get by a brutal approach. You must invite them." I wonder . . . Do I force bulbs to bloom indoors in winter, or do I invite them by providing the right conditions? Do I try to force my grandson to eat lunch, or do I invite him? Do I force respect or do I invite it? There are, of course, some areas in life when compliance is enforced. But "there are many things in life that you cannot get by a brutal approach. You must invite them." Maybe I need to brush up on my life skills, loosen up, and relax.

29

The January that I graduated with my master's degree in Vermont, snowdrifts mounded up shoulder-high and icicles daggered down from roofs almost to the ground. My friends and I crossed the quad bundled in multiple layers, braving steel-cold air to get to the dining hall. I ducked my head and pushed through, focused only on reaching my destination.

Then I read Mary Oliver's essay "Wordsworth's Mountain" in her book Upstream. She saw the frosty winter landscape through a different lens. To her, winter says welcome. I tend to think of spring as the welcoming season, but Mary Oliver invited me into winter. "There is a rumor of total welcome among the frosts of the winter morning," she wrote. Welcome comes from two Old English words: will, meaning want or desire, plus cuman, meaning to come. So welcome means "I want you to come." It's not an off-handed, "We're open; feel free to enter" but an earnest, "Come in! You are wanted here." I could have slowed down a bit in that Vermont winter. I could have noticed more. I could have welcomed winter as it was welcoming me. I wish I had.

30

"The glacier flowed over its ground as a river flows over a boulder; and since it emerged from the icy sea as from a sepulcher it has been sorely beaten with storms; but from all those deadly, crushing, bitter experiences comes this delicate life and beauty, to teach us that what we in our faithless ignorance and fear call destruction is creation." – John Muir

So it is with winter's seeming destruction of trees and plants. It is part of creation.

31

My cat is such a creature of habit. At night, she prowls from room to room making sure we are tucked into bed. After that, she often jumps in bed with me. But at some point in the night, she pounces out of bed and prowls around downstairs, often ending up with a favorite toy, a string with a folded piece of paper tied to the end. She began to drag this toy upstairs every night in the middle of the night, ready to play. I do enjoy playing with her, watching her leap and scramble after the paper as I drag it along—but not at two in the morning. Fortunately, after I shushed her several nights in a row, she got the point. I think. She sometimes still brings the string upstairs, but she leaves it in the doorway as if to catch my attention and remind me that when morning comes, it will be playtime again.

FEBRUARY

1

Clean,
soft,
faintly warm,
sweetly fragrant,
the outdoors this morning
smells like inspiration.

– kh –

2

I've put off pulling up or trimming off the old dead stalks and stems in my garden. As I walked back to my house from the mailbox today, I realized that I'm really drawn to these dried leaves and stems and seed pods. My favorites are the ones that are a golden red-brown, like the canna stalks. Their large leaves are wilted and sagging like drooped shoulders on their tall, stiff stems. They stand there, faithful sentinels, overseeing my driveway. The creeping Jenny, now a golden rust color, cascades like a dried-leaf waterfall from the containers on the rail of my back deck. Frilly brown citronella leaves are curled inward. The brittle mandevilla vine leans on its stake, its leaves translucent in the setting sun. I'm in love with my winter garden.

3

At breakfast this morning, I looked out the window and saw my next-door neighbor's large, brown and black dog nose-to-the-ground on the other side of our iron bar fence. He held his black tail curved over his back. The tip of his tail was facing me. It was white. I had never noticed this white spot before, because I think it's only noticeable if you're standing directly behind—or in this case, in front—of the curve. I immediately thought of markings I've seen on other animals: a white star on a horse's forehead, a crescent moon on a calf's face. And I recently saw a picture of a dalmatian puppy whose black spots were shaped like hearts. What a joyful, amazing wonder our world is.

4

The winter evening settles down . . .
six o'clock.
The burnt-out ends of smoky days.

– T.S. Eliot –

The soft, sharp scent of smoke drifts from our neighbors' chimneys this evening, a cheerful, friendly, cozy smell, a gather-around smell, a summons to watch roaring flames flicker and settle into glowing coals, an invitation to reflect on important things or trivial things or nothing at all, resting at the burnt-out ends of smoky days.

5

[A]stonished Art
. . . the mad wind's night-work,
the frolic architecture of the snow.

– Ralph Waldo Emerson –

The sky is a soft, snow-morning blue. As I drink my coffee, the flakes begin falling, and within minutes, the deck is covered. Soon, a plump, white cushion tops the railings and a thick, frosty blanket covers the ground. The world is quiet except for two pairs of cardinals who feast at the feeders. They flit back and forth from the feeder to the snowy deck, where they hop around, leaving their ditto-shaped tracks in the snow. They are round, red, feathered ornaments on this snow-white day.

6

Through the hush'd air the whitening shower
descends,
At first thin wavering, til at last the flakes
Fall broad and wide and fast, dimming the day
With a continual flow. The cherished fields
Put on their winter robe of purest white.

– James Thomson –

7

It's been a while since I've studied the inside of a spoon, the concave side, to see myself reflected upside down. I vaguely remember learning that the upside-down image is created by the angles at which the light hits the spoon and reflects into our eyes. But I'm more interested in the wonder of it. Over my shoulder in the reflection, I see upside down windows. And through those upside-down windows, I see the snow. I am holding a spoonful of winter.

8

"In winter the stars seem to have rekindled their fires, the moon achieves a fuller triumph, and the

heavens wear a look of a more exalted simplicity." –
John Burroughs

Look up at the sky. How far do you think we can
see? Maybe all the way to eternity.

9

Snowshine in full moon
at two a.m., bright as day.
Silent neighbors sleep.

– kh –

10

Can a quilt be knitted? I think maybe not. Strictly
speaking, a quilt is two layers of cloth sewn together
with down or batting in between. I have some frayed
quilts that are almost fifty years old now, stitched
together by my husband's grandmother who lived on
a farm in rural Tennessee. What I have made is not
like these. But maybe it's something akin to a quilt: a
knitted blanket. I made it out of thick yarn, knitting
one eight-inch square at a time. Then I stitched the
squares together. Like a quilt. A one-layer quilt. Of
thick yarn. And if I'm not strict about it—can a quilt
be knitted? I think maybe so.

11

Profoundly still the twilight air,
Lifeless the landscape; so we deem,
Till like a phantom gliding near
A stag bends down to drink the stream.

And far away a mountain zone,
A cold, white waste of snow-drifts lies,
And one star, large and soft and lone,
Silently lights the unclouded skies.

– Charlotte Bronte –

12

Today is a breath of fresh air—warm fresh air. But I'm too experienced with this touch-and-go weather of spring in midwinter to think that spring is actually at our doorstep. No, spring is just teasing us. It's weeks away from settling in. Still, it is coming, and that anticipation gives me a deep, satisfied feeling of hope. Winter is whispering its secret: "I'm not here to stay."

13

You are a bold one,
bright daffodil,
first to open.
You hold wide your petals
like arms welcoming every drop
of late-winter sun.
Your companions are still asleep
or too timid to peek out,
but here you are leading the way
and gladdening my heart,
for tomorrow, winter's frosty breath
will return.
But you have given me
a vision of spring
to see me through.

– kh –

14

Love is very simple
and amazingly complicated.
Love is easy,
and it's the hardest thing I've ever done.
Love is an uplifting joy
and a crushing sorrow.

Love makes me strong
but extremely vulnerable.
Love threads through my highest aspirations
and my deepest regrets.
Love is one of the great wonders of the world.

– kh –

15

Author André Gide wrote, "One doesn't discover new lands without consenting to lose sight of the shore for a very long time."

Questions
beckon us forward,
answers unknown,
mysteries unsolved,
uncertainties untamed.
But there's a drift of light
ahead in the dark,
a drift of hope in the doubt.
I don't sprint toward it,
though some do.
I don't even plod steadily on,
though some do.
I tiptoe,
squint toward the mist,
carry the questions,
and wonder
if there truly are
answers.

– kh –

16

Late lies the wintry sun a-bed,
A frosty, fiery sleepy-head;
Blinks but an hour or two; and then,
A blood-red orange, sets again.

– Robert Louis Stevenson –

For some reason, when the year tiptoes toward spring, I remember poems read to me in my childhood from a set of orange Childcraft books. Actually, it's the illustrations that I remember first and then the words and the feelings they stirred in me. I'm not even sure I can describe the feelings—warmth, peace, serenity, possibility, hope, goodness, the feeling of there's-a-whole-big-beautiful-world-out-there-for-me-to-experience. Maybe it's called wonder.

17

Settled. I like that word. It makes me feel . . . well, settled. I picture swirling flakes in a shaken snow globe as they come to rest. Or falling leaves, easing into a drift on the ground. Or feathers shaken from a pillow, floating lightly through the air to a gentle landing. They settle. I breathe in. I breathe out. I let

my shaken soul, my drifting thoughts, my tumbled
feelings settle.

18

O Wind,
if Winter comes,
can Spring be far behind."

– Percy Bysshe Shelley –

My dear Winter, you are a fine season. But,
honestly, I am looking forward to your warmer sister,
Spring.

19

As my grandson played on the swings in my yard
today, I pulled weeds in the garden, where they'd
taken over for the winter, spreading low and wide. I
had left them until now, because they were greenery
for days when everything else was washed in tones of
brown and gray. But it's time to make way for spring-
blooming plants, perennials that hopefully made it
through the winter. As I pulled up one of the last
clumps of weeds, it emerged cradling a millipede
coiled in sleep. Surely it was too early in the season
to wake up this rust and black-striped creature, and

yet . . . maybe? I called my grandson to come and look. We took the millipede to a sunny spot and carefully laid it there. In a moment, it uncurled and stretched and step-step-step-step-stepped along, traveling at a slow and steady pace. My grandson gathered pine straw and dirt and sticks to welcome this little friend. Fascinated, we watched him for at least an hour before we set him back in the dirt to finish his nap.

20

Spring is on the way soon, I think. I know the groundhog saw his shadow earlier this month, and I groaned. I am not a cold-weather person, and while I love a good snow, I love it from indoors looking out a window and warming myself with a hot cup of coffee or cocoa. But today is a milder day, and I'm hearing birds—not just the usual winter cardinals but other birds. The voices in this chorus are more varied and their symphony is fuller. I think they're singing of warmer weather and flowering plants and budding trees coming soon. So never mind the groundhog. I'm listening to the birds.

21

My yard is blooming with daffodils. I admire one close up, thinking of how it reminds me of a little dancer dressed in sunny yellow. And I realize that my yellow daffodils are the exact color of yes. (In my mind, some words come in colors.) So I have a yard full of yes. Which is delightful. Yes is an open door, an open window, open arms, an invitation. Creativity and discovery appear with yes. A bright yellow yes.

(In case you're curious: no is midnight blue. One is baby blue, two is pink, three is yellow, four is green, five is red, six is blue, seven is violet, eight is orange, nine is black. Hope is bluish white. Dinner is dark brown. It's a colorful world!)

22

There's a certain slant of light,
Winter Afternoons—
That oppresses like the Heft
Of Cathedral Tunes.

– Emily Dickinson –

Enough said.

23

From my sunroom at night, the outside world is reduced to squares of yellow light from the neighbors' windows, the eyes of houses that close their lids, now this one, now that, until all the houses are sleeping and my sunroom is no longer a sunroom at all but a dark cocoon lit only by the moon.

24

The huge great clouds move slowly, gently, as
Reluctant the quick sun should shine in vain, . . .
In all the myriad grey,
In silver height and dusky deep, remain
The loveliest
Faint purple flushes of the unvanquished sun.

– John Freeman –

I love the way the sun brightens the world even when the whole sky is covered with clouds. The sunlight is softer, cooler with cloud cover. Still, it wakes the world and keeps us company all day.

25

Robins are visiting my back deck this morning. Bright-eyed, they tilt their dark heads, drink from the birdbath, then flutter to the ground, puff their orange chests, and peck around. Spring . . . is coming?

26

Before a meal at home, I say, "Itadakimasu." It's an expression that my older son and his Japanese wife taught my husband and me. It means "I receive with gratitude." My son and his family say it before each meal to express thanks for everyone who provided the food on their table. This morning it occurred to me that I could say it as I rise and greet the day. For all the gifts this day will bring, itadakimasu.

27

Sunrise
sends a long, narrow streak of gold
flowing down my street
past spring-hopeful yards,
moving like a slow river.

– kh –

28

The clouds are showering us with snow today. It's coming down in fine feathery flakes that remind me of a Mother Goose rhyme:

> A pillow shaken in the sky,
> see how all the feathers fly,
> little snowflakes soft and light
> make the trees and meadows white.

29

> Oh, Spring is surely coming,
> Her couriers fill the air;
> Each morn are new arrivals,
> Each night her ways prepare;
> I scent her fragrant garments,
> Her foot is on the stair.

– John Burroughs –

Gardening wisdom in Tennessee tells us not to plant until the fifteenth of April. It's hard to wait. But while we can't plant, we can plan, for Spring's foot is on the stair.

MARCH

1

Daffodils,
that come before the swallow dares,
and take the winds of March with beauty.

– Shakespeare –

Our daffodils always begin blooming in February. They're courageous flowers, pushing through the snow, bowing to the cold rain, shuddering in the wind. The crocuses are early bloomers too. Their small, purple-petaled cups lie scattered across the grass under the magnolia, offering their cheery orange centers to the day. They always surprise me when they appear. "Here we are again," they seem to say, "We've not forgotten you. And neither has spring."

2

The geese are back.
I heard their voices
honking
as if there were a traffic jam
in the sky.
But there were only the geese

skimming the air,
aimed straight and steady,
wings gently flapping,
honking and waving
to those of us
grounded below.

– kh –

3

Today was sunny, on the edge between warm and cool, which made it just right for taking my youngest grandson to the zoo. We stroked a silky-soft kangaroo, caught a glimpse of a sun-bathing Andean bear, and watched the always-alert meerkats as they watched us. And, of course, we bought a souvenir: a battery-operated bubble blower shaped like a dinosaur head. It was great at making loads of bubbles, which we did immediately. Iridescent blue, green, and yellow bubbles rolled out, bobbed in the breeze, and got caught up in puffs of invisible air currents that carried them as high as the treetops. When we left the zoo, we opened all the windows in the car, and through the traffic all the way home, we left clouds of glorious bubbles in our wake.

4

At twilight this evening, a perfect thunderstorm rolled in. We've not had one like this in a long time. It arrived with very little wind, a steady showering rain, and rolling thunder that rumbled and drummed the air, bumping and grumbling and growling and taking its time. The deep-throated grumble gradually grew distant but sent back one last afterthought, an echoing, tumbling tirade. Then it moved on, leaving tips and taps of rain and a sky deepening toward night.

5

My cat jumped into my lap just now, and as I ran my fingers through her silver-gray fur, I remembered something I haven't thought of in years: a muff. When I was five or six, I carried a muff in cold weather. My little sister had one too, a white, furry pillow-like hand warmer. They were the size of a little-girl purse but with a tunnel through the middle where you put both your hands on a cold, cold day. We wore wool church-coats and white furry ear muffs to match the muffs we held at our waist, both hands inside like demure young ladies, although we were much too young to be even the youngest of ladies. I am now among the oldest of ladies. And here in my lap is—

well, not a muff, but she's just as good for warming me on this cold, late winter night.

6

These are the days when Birds come back—
A very few—a Bird or two—
To take a backward look.

– Emily Dickinson –

7

Joy in looking and comprehending
is nature's most beautiful gift.

– Albert Einstein –

The moon is halfway to full tonight. Clouds stretch across it in a thin, ragged veil that gathers the moonlight into a glowing circle surrounding it. Rimming the edge of this circle, all the way around, is a faint rainbow. For some time, I stand beneath it, gazing up. I want to hold it in my mind and tuck it into my heart, tonight's gift.

8

Sun-dimming,
cloud-skimming,
darkening skies,
thundery
wondery,
wind on the rise.
Raindrops
in fat plops
and lightning—surprise!
There's a flash
and a crash,
and the cat streaks inside.

– kh –

9

The hills are a hazy purple this morning as the sun rises. I watch as they lighten moment by moment to a soft, misty gray that deepens to a blue violet. I see these hills through the lacework of winter-bare branches, and I want to take them in, into my mind, my soul, my spirit. I want to hold them in my memory, for with spring approaching and the branches swelling with the buds and blossoms, I know I won't see these hills from my window until next winter. As much as I welcome spring, I will miss this view of the hills.

10

Filmy clouds
skim the deep blue
in a stately
take-your-time
procession.

– kh –

11

I finally discovered the name of the purple, bunched up, ruffled flowers that often come in the bouquets I buy at the grocery store. Blue statice. They stay fresh-looking and bright long after the other blooms have withered. Even after they dry and get brittle and prickly, they keep their color. I found out that they're picked before the blooms are fully open, which keeps them compact and ruffly. I have blue statice in an arrangement on my kitchen counter right now. When the rest of the flowers droop, I'll put them in the compost. But the blue statice I'll keep. On the windowsill above my sink, a small glass vase waits.

12

Plump little robin
dipping into the birdbath
for a sip of heated water
on this crisp-cold
cloudless day,
have you come to say
spring is near?
Not here,
not yet,
but near?
Now your friend lands beside you,
and you both,
with white-circled eyes,
look around and then fly.
Stay.
Stay, little redbreast.
Help me dream of spring.

– kh –

13

Today the sky is full of soft gray clouds lined in brilliant white where the sunlight touches them. Trees are still, birds puff up their feathers to stay warm. For a moment, the world is quiet and tranquil. It's an interesting word, tranquil. The Latin tranquillus means "quiet, calm, still." Tranquil makes me think of a lake so still and unruffled that it reflects the sky above and the trees on its shore, creating a mirror image. I wish to be a tranquil soul, unruffled, a mirror image of peace. In moments like this, observing the clouds, breathing deeply, opening my heart to the gifts of the day, it's not hard to feel tranquil.

14

Film producer Sam Goldwyn said, "If I look confused, it's because I'm thinking." A joke among writers is that we spend a lot of time sitting around staring into space and get to call it work. And most of the time, it actually is work. Batting ideas around in our minds. Considering. Picking up one thought. Putting it down. Picking up another thought. Putting it down only to pick up the first thought again. Who knows exactly how creativity works? I just know that reflecting is essential to the process. Pair it with thoughtfulness, and it's essential to peace.

15

A door is what a dog is perpetually on the wrong side of.

– Ogden Nash–

When I dogsat over a long weekend for my son and his family, I spent much of the time letting the dogs in and letting the dogs out. I do the same for my cat, but she's catty about it. When I open the door to let her inside, she'll often sit there, peering in. Then she'll turn her back and casually stroll away. If there were a thought bubble above her head, I think it would say, "Just checking to make sure the door still opens."

16

How do you eat sunshine and wind and rain? It's a riddle of a question, and it came to me during a choir rehearsal at church as we prepared for a Celtic service. One of our songs, a Celtic prayer, began, "Be gentle when you touch bread."

> Be gentle when you touch bread,
> let it not lie uncared for,
> taken for granted or unwanted.
> There is such beauty in bread,
> beauty of sun and soil,
> beauty of patient toil . . .
> Winds and rain,
> Winds and rain . . .
> There is such beauty in bread.
>
> – a Celtic prayer –

How do you eat sunshine and wind and rain? By eating bread.

17

Magenta. Purplish red. It's not a color I wear, not a color I usually paint with. But I was inspecting a box of pastels that I've had for ages, and there in the upper left-hand corner was a stick of magenta. And I thought of Grandmother, my father's mother. She died when I was twelve, so my memories of her are from my childhood. She loved wearing costume jewelry, and she wore magenta. Not always, of course, but when I see magenta, I think of her. It's interesting the way a color, maybe even a particular shade of color, can become a mode of time travel, carrying us into a memory. Today magenta is taking me back in time.

18

The entire morning sky
was melon colored
with a splash of lemon
at the eastern horizon,
a welcome to this cloud-covered day.
I made my bed
and looked out again.
The melon and lemon
(both with the same letters)
were gone, replaced
by the softest blue.
I know the bright melon lemon sun
is somewhere above,
rising higher and higher,
but we below are now tented
by this blue
that darkens into gray.

And then comes the rain.

– kh –

19

Out my upstairs window, past the bobbing branches of pines and the tangle of naked winter branches, oak and elm and hackberry, one tree on the next block stands out over the rooftops in a plume of white. A Bradford pear, most likely. Overnight, spring has dressed her in this finery, her "Sunday Best" as we used to say. For tomorrow is Sunday. But maybe it's a birthday gift. For tomorrow is also the first day of spring.

20

Architecture in general is frozen music.

– Friedrich von Schelling –

The thought of architecture as music has me looking more closely at buildings around town, asking myself what kind of music I'm seeing. Some buildings seem to be grand symphonies. Others are jazzy or like Japanese pop, easy listening, or golden oldies. But in my own neighborhood, it's hard to separate the architecture from the people who live there. Knowing the neighbors seems to color my view of the houses. Are they a jazzy family? An orderly march? A lullaby? And what about Nature's architecture—hills, valleys, grasslands, canyons, cliffs, beaches? Maybe all the world is a grand song being sung out into the universe.

21

Everything that exists is in a manner the seed of that which will be.

– Marcus Aurelius –

It amazes me how seeds are so different, from tiny black poppy seeds to large tan avocado pits, from flat smooth mango seeds to prickly peach pits. Once when I taught four-year-olds, I was sharing the wonders of seeds with them, and I said that even bananas have seeds. I broke a banana in half and pointed out the tiny black dots in the center. Then I passed around banana slices for everyone to eat. One little boy refused to eat any, because he now knew a terrible truth: Bananas have seeds!

22

I'm at home right now—not my childhood home but my grownup home. It's a colorful, comfortable place, a good and familiar place. But in a way, the deepest and richest home is inside me.

I carry my home in my heart,
a sense of wide, western sunsets,
of expansive life,
of nature's joy,
of childhood delight.
Home is a spring-like window of the soul
opening to renaissance,
to possibility,
unfolding like a perfumed bloom.
Home is a deep breath,
fresh air
and fullness of hope
that looks ahead
toward new paths yet to be hiked,
new vistas yet to be viewed,
new and ever-changing skies,
and the inviting golden glow
over the horizon.

– kh –

23

My study of drawing has once again challenged how I look at the world. The artist Kimon Nicolaides wrote that instead of the edge of a figure being a line, it's "in reality simply the place where the figure ceases to exist." I'd been looking at lines all around me, seeing them as horizontal, vertical, diagonal, squiggly, jagged, curved. But real-life lines are not really lines. They're the edges or curving sides of three-dimensional beings or objects. So now I'm seeing edges not as lines but as a continuation of the dimensions of something or someone. Seeing in this way connects to a sense of touch, even if I'm not touching what I'm looking at. I feel the shape in my hands, on my palms, under my fingers. Will that new way of seeing translate into drawing? I don't know. But it's changing the way I see.

24

My youngest grandson spent most of this afternoon on backyard safari, hunting pill bugs, aka roly-polies. We lifted one flower pot after another and found whole colonies of the skittering, segmented, multi-legged black creatures. To my grandson, we were the search and rescue team. He filled a plastic box with dirt, moistened the dirt to make it pliable, and molded it into hills and valleys. Then he rescued the little bugs from under the flowerpots and re-homed them to his dirt-filled box, where he watched them, delighted with his roly-poly pets. It was an afternoon of anticipation and discovery, and as I watched him watch bugs, I was delighted too.

25

I learned a new old word today from editor Victoria Griffin: bochord. It's an old word for a library, and it means "book hoard." That seems totally appropriate. In fact, I think it might describe my house.

26

The movement of bodies
is a wonder.
Hand bones,
wrist bones,
toe bones,
knees and shoulders—
it's a wonder
that these should carry us,
hinge us,
brace us—
or not.

Having fallen, I know
a bit
about the absence of agility,
which makes the wonder
of well-working limbs
and neck and backbone
stand out
(if I may say it that way).
The ease of movement,
the tiptoe,
the jog,
the reach,
the downward dog,
the dance,
the climb,
the bend,
the stretch—
the movement of bodies
is a wonder.

– kh –

27

This morning, the sky looked like a plowed field striped with ridge-rows of clouds. Each ridge was one long line of cloud, white along the leading edge, easing to gray-blue at the rear. Between each ridge ran a strip of bright blue morning sky. The whole field

drifted slowly east. Maybe it will bring someone a
harvest of rain.

28

In the early morning sunshine,
a robin perches
on the tip-top peak
of my neighbor's roof
and stands so still
he looks like a statue,
a roof ornament.
He looks like
the King of Spring.

– kh –

29

My candle burns at both ends;
It will not last the night;
But ah, my foes, and oh, my friends—
It gives a lovely light.

– Edna St. Vincent Millay –

Some days, I feel like Millay wrote this poem by reading my mind. I guess some things never change. What keeps my candle burning? A good chunk of solitude "and oh, my friends."

30

The wind is passing through today,
whistling like an old friend
all in a rush to cover ground,
to get somewhere,
though who knows where?
I recognize its whistle and whine
as it slips through screens
at the open window
and swoops past power lines
letting them know
who really has the power here.

– kh –

31

Time changes everything,
except something within us
which is always surprised by change.

– Thomas Hardy –

One of the things I love about nature is the way it changes. Shadows lengthen, shorten, sharpen, soften, and disappear altogether. Day changes to night and night to day. Storm clouds move on, changing the day from rainy to sunny. A stream changes into a river, which changes into the sea. When I travel across the country, flatlands change into hills and mountains. And when I'm home, every morning, every afternoon, and every evening, from my windows, I get to see nature create a different painting of sky and trees, birds and weather. I get to see winter change to spring.

SPRING

APRIL

From my kitchen window this morning,
I spied you dancing with your partner,
your wings a blur of gray and white.
You faced each other,
fluttering up a foot or so
then fluttering down to the ground.
After a brief rest,
feathers whipped out once more,
you took a short whirl together.
Now you perch on a fence post,
white breasts, soft gray backs,
gray wings striped with white.
You both rise again in a flirty, fluttery swirl of wings.
A pudgy squirrel scampers out of your way
as you once again drift to the ground,
but you pay him no attention
as you continue your spring fling.

Later, I see you watching me through my window.
Asking me to dance?
Why, yes, thank you, I believe I will.
And if I could,
I would fly.

– kh –

2

I broke a glass pitcher—and I mean I shattered it to smithereens. It was sitting on my counter when I pulled a bowl out of the cabinet above it. The bowl slipped and hit the pitcher, and glass exploded. Small shards flew everywhere, nearby and across the room. Even after I swept, tiny pieces kept showing up as I moved and a different slant of light glittered on stray shards. Some things show up only in the right slant of light. Rainbows. Reflections in water. Sparkles on stone. Dust on furniture. And broken glass.

3

O! it is pleasant, with a heart at ease
Just after sunset, or by moonlight skies,
To make the shifting clouds be what you please . . .

– Samuel Taylor Coleridge –

Sunset this evening bathed the western edge of our gray clouds with a brilliant pink color that held an edge of gold. In contrast, the sky beyond and above the cloud was a clear, deepening blue. I've long thought that if I tried to paint a sky with those colors, people would shake their heads and call it unrealistic. I went to get my camera to capture the proof of those colors, but when I returned, the pink had faded. I felt almost as if I had imagined it. But no, it had truly been one of those brilliant pink and gold evenings. I have captured it in my memory.

4

On my desk, I keep a jar candle that a friend gave me. It's made of tiny pieces of red glass arranged in a jumbled fashion, each piece angled so that its facets reflect the candlelight inside. In the darkness, it's flame-sparked, deeper red where the glass is thicker and brighter where the glass is thin, throwing the edges of each tiny piece into contrast. Even in sunlight, without its candle burning, the jar glows red like rubies. Red like wine. Red like cherry hard candies. Red like cranberries. The deep, rich color of friendship.

5

Beating heart—
beating with the growth
of greening things,
diving and alive,
swimming in color,
finding space,
leaving space,

reflecting,
traveling,
circling,
rounding
vision of hope.
Beating,
beating,
beating
heart.

– kh –

6

"Some of the flour got on my feet. And some got on my dinosaur," my grandson explained. We were baking bread. I assured him that messes are part of cooking—or any kind of making. And we can clean up. Isn't that the way of life—making messes, cleaning up messes, and ending up at the dinner table eating hot, buttered homemade rolls.

7

Blooms
dancing in the breeze;
it's all I ask for,
it's all I need.

And when my ashes
are scattered on the ground,
it's all I hope to feed.

– kh –

8.

New, yellow-green leaves on the hackberry form a tiny, frilly fringe along the thin, crooked branches. A jet skims past high above the newly budding trees, crossing just beneath the pale blue-gray cloud cover, the soft leading edge of the rain to come. "Nature is your book of reference," said Frank Lloyd Wright, "and in it you study and learn." I am learning again about the patient unfolding of spring.

9

There's a snowy look
to the low, gray clouds.
I don't want to complain, but
"Wait!" I say. "It's April."
The hackberry has unfolded
this year's new leaves,
the wine-rich redbuds are full of blooms,
the cherries are already
shedding their spent blossoms,

white and pink and delicate,
a carpet of springtime
gracing the lawn,
flecking the driveway.
Yet old man winter has come back
for one last fling before spring.

Winter's breath has brought
a slog of snow-laden clouds
that hover and cover the spring-hopeful trees.
As the wind picks up,
it scatters sleet,
hurls it at windows and walkways
and wrens who dart for cover.
Did they sense snow coming?
Did the brisk breeze foretell it?
Or are they as startled as I?
Are they under the eaves,
tucked beneath new leaves,
complaining, "Wait! It's April"?

– kh –

10

Snow fell in a dusting of white that's melting quickly in the warmth of the sun. Chickadees twitter, a squirrel races up a pine tree, and there's a scent of freshness in the air, an assurance of spring. Nature nudges us to notice, to pay attention with all our senses, and when we do, she rewards us with wonder.

11

Before I rise, I take a deep breath, grateful for a new day.

New, as in reappearing. Like the wild violets that cover my yard in the spring. A new one appeared this week, tipped with droplets of rainwater that sparkled in the sunlight.

New, as in existing for the first time. Like the paintings that I plan to create in art class this week, expressions of my soul that have never been seen before.

New, as in unfamiliar. Maybe I'll surprise myself.

New, as in starting over. As I will do tomorrow morning and the next morning and the next morning, beginning again and again for the rest of my life.

12

My husband spent a good part of the day repairing the deck stairs. He sawed the wood in the basement, and the scent drifted around the house, soft and warmly sweet. When it's all repaired, maybe I should ask him to make a daily habit of sawing wood in the basement. It makes a delightful air freshener.

13

Bumblebee hovering
between house and hedgerow,
are you really hovering,
or are you trying to make progress
against the gusty wind?

– kh –

14

"Mountains and oceans have whole worlds of innumerable wondrous features. We should understand that it is not only our distant surroundings that are like this, but even what is right here, even a single drop of water." – Dogen Zenji

Sometimes I pour bubble bath into the kitchen sink to fill it with suds for my grandson to play in. He mounds the suds into mountains and fills cups with it, dipping and pouring to his heart's content. He's not here today, but I felt adventurous, so I stood at the sink and filled a coffee cup with bubble bath soap and a bit of water. Then I stuck a straw into it and blew. Big bubbles heaped up, overflowed the cup, and dripped into the kitchen sink (where I was standing). The more I blew, the more bubbles mounded up. Their tops were rounded, but the sides where they connected were flat. Although they were transparent, they sparkled with little winks of color—red, yellow, blue, and green. And because the sun was shining straight through the window, each bubble wore a small, bright, round reflection of the sun, complete with tiny rays all around it. It's now my humble opinion that bubbles have whole worlds of innumerable wondrous features.

15

I'll tell you how the sun rose
A ribbon at a time.

– Emily Dickinson –

The golden light of sunrise traces the outstretched branches of the budding elm and kisses its topmost twigs with bright white. Their tips look like candle flames. Birds sing in joyful chips and chirps, whirrs and whistles. They seem overjoyed at the spreading warmth of the morning sun. It brightens the fresh green fringe of emerging leaves on the hackberry and splashes down onto pale lenten roses, lemon yellow forsythias, delicate white dogwoods, and showy pink azaleas. I step outside to sit in the sunrise, to soak in Spring, to be witness to birdsong and silent spreading leaves. They need no witness, of course, no audience. Witnessed or not, they share themselves with the world. It is I who need to hear their voices, to witness their steady, calm existence, their being, their embodiment of joy, their persistence. It is I who need this hope.

16

I was working at my desk this morning when I heard the sound of a drill outside. My first thought was that our neighbor was building or repairing something. But then I realized the sound was much closer than that. As I rose to look out the window, a bright red head bobbed into view. A woodpecker had been pecking at the gutter. He saw me just as I saw him—and he flew. I'm pretty sure he'll find a better lunch by pecking at a tree.

17

Who bends a knee where violets grow
A hundred secret things shall know.

– Rachel Field –

A warm spring breeze passes by, and the dogwood branches wave as if to say, "Here! Here! We have secrets to tell." Freckled, pink blooms of Lenten roses lean in. "Who told you?" The azalea fluffs her frilly blossoms. "The bees," she says. "The bees tell secrets." Newborn violets nod and whisper, "Yes. We heard." I kneel to look into their happy little violet faces. "What is the secret?" I ask. For a moment, all is quiet except for a finch chirping above and leaves shifting in the breeze. Then I hear it: "Some of us bloom, some of us buzz. We are all in it together." And that's only one of the hundred secrets a violet knows.

18.

For years fleet away with the wings of the dove.

– Lord Byron –

We used to have soft gray mourning doves in our yard. We grew used to hearing their mournful coos and watching them peck sunflower seeds that other birds dropped from the feeder. But then one year, the doves didn't return, at least not to our part of town. We had plenty of other birds. Brown thrashers dropped by. The rufous sided towhee visited from time to time. But not doves. Then this year, the doves came back, cooing and bobbing and pecking. If the years fleet away with the wings of the dove, do the years come back when the doves do?

19

I have an inflatable globe, the beach ball kind, and I blew it up so I could show my five-year-old grandson where his cousins live—California and before that, Japan. I also showed him where his other grandparents live, north of the Arctic Circle in Norway. I know this big wide world is hard to comprehend when you're five. Still, I think it's nice to know that the world is mapped, and we can pinpoint the place where these people are when we Facetime with them. Sometimes I think life is like a journey without a map. It's encouraging to know that I'm traveling with friends, and we're all heading toward the same horizon.

20

Creative minds are rarely tidy.

– unknown –

I dip the side of my right pinky finger into a small puddle of yellow paint that has a bit of red drifting into it from another puddle. Carefully, I touch the small square canvas with the tip of my pinky. Then I rock my finger back toward my hand and leave a print that looks like a flower petal, yellow with a streak of red. I dip the outside of my right arm, elbow to wrist into paint puddled in various colors on a large tray. Then I press my painted arm onto a large white sheet of paper. I swipe right like a windshield wiper and leave a rainbow. It feels good to get messy, to be allowed, even encouraged to. It makes me think of the black and white photograph of me at age three holding a piece of grape jelly-covered toast, grinning at the camera in delight, my mouth encircled by jelly. The joy of messiness. Maybe that doesn't change.

21

I was reading a book this evening, and seemingly from nowhere, here came an ant crossing the page, trekking from one line to another, one letter to the next, white space to black line, black line to white space. How big, I wondered, must those letters be to an ant? Monumental. Like crop circles that can only be seen from an airplane or drone. Shall I read it to you, little ant?

22

One of my joys is coming downstairs as some delicious aroma is wafting up, greeting me halfway. Like coffee in the morning. Or a baking potato as dinnertime nears. Or simmering soup. Or homemade rolls when company is coming. The moment invites deep breathing.

23

Our next-door neighbors had a yard sale last weekend. I didn't intend to go, because I didn't need anything, and I wanted to avoid the temptation to buy. So I contented myself to window shop—from my kitchen window. That's when I saw an easel. I actually needed an easel. I slipped on my shoes and

trundled over to see how much they wanted for it.
Five dollars. Yes. I needed that particular easel. Then
I saw some frames that I needed for my artwork. And
there, farther back, was a sort-of chest of drawers. The
three drawers were golden-brown baskets resting on
wooden shelves in an open sided, metal frame. And,
well, I needed that, too. I'm now sitting across the
room wondering exactly what I'll put in that chest of
baskets. Toys, I think, for when my grandkids visit.
Dinosaurs and trucks and cars, maybe even art
supplies—play dough, paint, pens, paper. I'm not
sure. I remember that the writer Madeleine L'Engle
said something like, "Inspiration comes during work,
not before." I know that once I start filling the basket-
drawers, I'll figure out what goes where. That's when
I'll be inspired.

24

Third star to the right and straight on toward
morning.

– J.M. Barry, *Peter Pan* –

The shadows were sharp
deep in the night,
the gibbous moon bright
and high in the sky,
one pinpoint planet nearby.

Trillions of stars
are out there somewhere
beyond these two,
but I see only the two
silently watching
this sleeping world
and me.
Or so I think
until
two blinking white lights
cross the sky
like twin roving stars,
a jet so high
I hear no sound
as it winks its way
past moon and planet.
Yes, others are awake—
those who fly across
this dark expanse,
and those like me
in the sharp shadows below,
watching
deep in the night.

– kh –

25

Colours seen by candle-light
Will not look the same by day.

– Elizabeth Barrett Browning –

We recently painted our kitchen gray. The hardest part might have been deciding which gray we wanted. Who knew there were so many variations on the theme? Blue-grays and gray-blues, almost-whites and almost-browns, steel and seal and dove and cloud and dozens more. We looked at the colors in different lights, squinted and imagined what a whole wall of cabinets would look like in one shade or another. We chose one to try on a single cabinet door and checked it in daylight and at night—it was too dark. Finally, we settled on a soft, warm gray. After all the back and forth and the angst around the choice, I call it the color of peace.

26

If you get simple beauty and naught else,
You get about the best thing God invents.

– Robert Browning –

The blue-purple dwarf irises have bloomed, and their cousins, the large bearded iris, look like they'll open soon as well. I think of May as their month, but these extravagant, perfumed ladies are perfectly welcome to come early to the spring garden party. When a plant blooms, it seems like it's celebrating itself. And why not? A flower's simple beauty is about the best thing God invents.

27

Is it true
that we all have a favorite chair?
I do.
Mine rocks,
an easy motion back and forth,
not a swing
but a gentle bounce,
a slow sway
like a cradle.
Perhaps it stirs
a deep, hidden memory
of my mother's arms,
of my grandmother's lap.
Is that why it soothes me,
makes me feel safe
and cared for
and carried?
Now I'm a grandmother.

No one soothes me,
no one carries me except this chair,
this settle-down snuggle-up
take-it-easy chair.
Is it true
that we all have a favorite chair?
I hope we do.

– kh –

28

I read recently that alert literally means *on the watchtower*. In Italy in the 16th century, the military commonly used the phrase *stare all' erta*, meaning to stand on the watchtower. Eventually, it came to simply mean *stand watch*, and as words and phrases do, it morphed into something shorter. Now, in English, it's just *alert*. On watch. From my bedroom windows above my desk, looking out and down from the second story, I sometimes feel that I stand on a watchtower. I look out onto the roofs and windows of neighboring houses, over elms and hackberries, oaks and maples, crape myrtle and pines, hostas and dogwoods and azaleas. And birds, too—robins and cardinals, wrens and finches, chickadees and titmice and mockingbirds. This is the realm over which I stand watch, alert to the changing seasons, the shifting cloudscapes, the dance of nature.

29

O chestnut tree, great-rooted blossomer,
Are you the leaf, the blossom, or the bole?
O body swayed to music, O brightening glance,
How can we know the dancer from the dance?

– William Butler Yeats –

For many of us, music is not just what we make or listen to but what we move to. Maybe that's a statement of common knowledge for some people, but for those of us who were taught that dancing is a sin, it's a statement of discovery. For some of us, music seeps into our bones, nudges our muscles, beats in our hearts, and tilts our heads. We sway. We glance. Eventually, we have to dance, to express ourselves in ballet, jazz, waltz . . . How can we know the dancer from the dance? We can't, not when it's in the soul. When it's in the soul, the dancer is the dance, and the dance is the dancer.

30.

Spring teases in turns
through warm and cold and warm again,
winter then spring then winter again,
and just when I despair

that she has forgotten us this year, she
springs!
She buds and blossoms,
opens her heart colors,
her rainbow hues,
her humming bugs,
her budding branches,
bright even in the rinsing rain
and rumbling thunder,
even in the breezy mild air
that says, "Warm, warm,
warm up the world."
And the birds—oh my!—
robins and finches, doves and mockingbirds
flit and fly on the wind,
dive in, peck around
swirl and swoop and sing their enchantments.
The columbine nods in answer.
Windflowers shift and sway in a dance.
Spring! Spring!
The outburst of spring!

– kh –

MAY

1

Hello, May. What an interesting name you have. Yours is a name of possibility: you may enter, you may dream, you may dance. Your name is a wish, a prayer—may you be at peace, may you have joy. You are a springtime festival. You are the bridge to summer. You are a flowering month, a singing month, a month of ends and beginnings. Hello, May. What an interesting month you are.

2

A slow, gentle rain
flicks the leaves of the honeysuckle,
glazes the petals of impatiens,
rests in droplets on arching iris leaves.
When the rain slows to a mist,
I step outside,
stand in the shelter
of a crape myrtle,
and inhale the scent
of rain-washed air
and rich, wet earth.
Then a playful gust of wind
whips through the yard,

> sending a shower of rainwater
> from the tree,
> which sends me
> back indoors
> to dry off.

-kh

3

I was studying my folded hands, the way the fingers intertwine, how they hug, how the palms press together, how the two become one unit, how this can be a sign of prayer, the left linked into the right and the right linked into the left. And I thought of how good it is to have friends, to clasp hands, to walk the road together, to link arms, to stand shoulder to shoulder or sit cross-legged knee to knee—even if only figuratively. Friends are the hands folded, the high five. Friends hand off a baton, pass a talking stick, pick up a burden. Friends open a door, even if only one of them can walk through.

4

An artist friend hosted an exhibit of her work a few months ago. Since I was helping to lead a writing group in the gallery that day, I asked each of the participants to find a painting and study it, to let it speak to all their senses, to be conscious of their inner response to it, and then write what they felt. I chose a painting with a viewpoint that looked down from above to a coast below, the sea beyond, and birds soaring the skies. "I'm flying over the land," I wrote, "over inlets of ocean in the far north. I taste the freshness of the air, crisp and cold and smoky. I smell the brine and the dirt, rich and loamy, and the forests below. The scents draw me toward morning, the light of daybreak over the sea. I fly above it all, hearing the breakers and the far-off calls of water birds, who are surprised to see me up here. They flock toward me but then wheel away, for I am strange and solitary and light as feathers buoyed by a sea of air."

5

There's a beekeepers' saying that comes from the mid-seventeenth century: "A swarm in May is worth a load of hay; a swarm in June is worth a silver spoon; but a swarm in July is not worth a fly." I guess that's a beekeeper's way of saying, "To everything there is a season."

6

Silence is part of
song.
Negative space is part of
design.
Fear is part of
courage.
Uncertainty is part of
moving forward.
Doubt is part of
faith.
All these moving parts—
doubt and faith,
moving forward in uncertainty,
courage in fear,
negative beside positive,
silence within song—
all these are
the realities of
Life.

– kh –

7

Blue bachelor's buttons have bloomed in my wildflower garden, and I'm delighted. I went to my flower book to find out more about them and discovered that these particular blooms are cornflowers. But really, any ragged-edged flower can be called a bachelor's button. It seems that at one time, when covered buttons were the fashion in mens' clothing, bachelors' buttons—the real kind of buttons—were often worn and ragged at the edge. So people casually—maybe even as a joke, who knows—began to call any ragged-edged flower a bachelor's button. Maybe it was a put-down, but I can't think of anything nicer than being associated with a pretty flower.

8

Sadness is a river,
a rivulet of rain.
Grief is an ocean
lapping at the shore,
swelling as the tide comes in.

– kh –

9

Even the rainbow has a body
made of drizzling rain
and it is an architecture of glistening atoms
built up, built up
yet you can't lay your hand on it,
nay, nor even your mind.

– D.H. Lawrence –

There are very few clouds in the sky today, but there's a rainbow on my bathroom floor and up the wall. We have a new window covering in an etched-glass design of flowers, and it splits the sunlight into colors as it passes through. This array of colors, this fanned-out light, is a pleasant surprise. A rainbow is a show-stopper. Its appearance calls for a pause, a moment of reverence, maybe because it's not an everyday occurrence, at least not where I live. And it's fleeting. You miss it if you don't look up at the right time. Or in this case, if you don't look down and sideways.

10

There are some things you learn best in calm, and some in storm.

– Willa Cather –

My youngest grandson was upset with me. You could say that the emotional atmosphere was a bit stormy. The reason? I had hidden a surprise for him and tried to make a game of challenging him to find it. But I hadn't told him what the surprise was. That wouldn't upset some kids; they'd just look around and try to find something unusual or surprising in the familiar setting. But no, that wouldn't do here, and I learned something. In fact, my grandson told me to write it down so I would remember: "Tell what the surprise is before asking me to look for it." Got it.

11

We had a family cookout this evening. My sister and brother-in-law came, and both my sons and their families were here. As I sliced onions in the kitchen, I listened to the voices rising and falling in laughing, animated waves from the back deck. My sister was gathering ketchup and mustard to take outside—until I sliced a tomato. I must have looked astonished, because my sister leaned in, and we both stared at the insides of the tomato. It looked like it was full of worms. Plural. Lots of tiny, skinny, curly, green worms. "Oh dear," I said. Or maybe she said it. Or maybe we both said it at once. She whipped out her phone and did a fast search. "It's sprouts," she said, holding out the phone so I could see the picture. It seems that tomato seeds can sprout inside a perfectly good tomato. We were both stunned. And since it was a rare tomato—a sprouted one—and the only tomato I had, I went ahead and sliced the rest and served it. Sprouts are good for you, I've heard.

12

A few sunflower seeds spilled on the deck this morning when I refilled the bird feeder. I leave spilled seeds for chipmunks and squirrels and birds that prefer their food on the ground. Sure enough, in a while, here came a chipmunk, a little bundle of gold-brown fur with a long tail and two stripes down his back. He scooped up the stray seeds and stuffed them all in his cheek pouches before scampering away. Later he showed up at the full-length window of my back door. He stood on his hind legs, peered in, and squeaked twice. Looking for seeds? He shifted to the left and stood again, looked in, and squeaked. I have bad news for him. My cat is out there somewhere. Scamper away, little chipmunk. Scamper away. There's a silver-gray predator nearby.

13

It's a small restaurant,
crowded with young professionals
and college students
and my son

and his young family.
I nod to the tables
filled with younger people
talking and laughing
and dreaming
over lunch.
"The world is theirs."
I remark this to my son,
who is, of course,
of a younger generation.
He says,
"You've still got a lot to contribute."
I appreciate the sentiment.
I do.
Because I know
I have more to give
if given the time.
But I think what I was saying is,
"The world is yours now."
I was letting him know
that I have no problem
handing him the baton,
for the world is theirs.
The future is theirs.
And I'm happy to hand it over—
with apologies.
They'll do better than my generation.
I'm confident of that.

– kh –

14

I once researched the structure of castles in order to write some fantasy novels. I learned that a castle's strongest and most secure building was called a keep. It was a place you could go for safety if you were being attacked. Sometimes the jail was the keep. Fascinated by the word keep, I took a short detour to the dictionary and found that the verb keep has dozens of definitions: maintain, stay with, persist, sustain, remain in, preserve, embrace, support, tend, guard, defend, comply with, respect, celebrate, support, nurture, nourish. Being an explorer of words, I wondered if those definitions would broaden my understanding of the phrase "keep quiet." What does keep quiet mean?

Maintain quiet. Stay with it. Persist in it. Sustain it.
Remain in it.
Preserve quiet. Embrace it. Support it. Tend it. Guard
it. Defend it.
Respect quiet. Celebrate it. Support it. Nurture it.
Nourish it.
Shhh.
Keep Quiet.

15

After lunch yesterday, I simply sat in my sunroom. I would say I sat in silence, but while I was silent, the world around me kept humming—a gentle tick of the clock, the soft breath of the air conditioner, muted chirps from birds outdoors, the distant rush of a jet crossing the sky. Sunlight turned the tops of the leaves outside a bright green, while deeper in and underneath, the leaves lay in a forest of dark shadow. A gentle breeze swayed the stems of windflowers and black-eyed Susans, leading them in a slow dance. I was still and silent for only a moment, but that moment filled me with a sense of expanding serenity. I returned to the tasks of the day refreshed and hopeful.

16

I bought a whole cabbage today for the first time in ages. Or maybe I should say "a head of cabbage." It's firm and round in my hands and resembles a head, which is where it got its name—from the old French word for head, caboche, which in turn came from Latin caput, also meaning head. Anyway, my son and his family are visiting, and my Japanese daughter-in-law wants to make a special dish that they like. They've shopped at a Japanese market here and have bought all the other special ingredients, including a particular kind of rice, a must-have for their recipes. I watch her cut the cabbage in half, then in fourths, exposing the layers of leaves inside. Then she chops it, angling the chunk of cabbage this way and that to get clean, precise slices. I realize in that moment that the careful preparation of this meal is a gift.

17

My three-year-old granddaughter loves lemons. She joyfully eats them without sugar or salt or anything to cut the sour. When she gnaws into the juicy segments, my mouth instinctively tightens, and I wrinkle my nose. A lemon is a puckery wonder.

18

Noticing something makes it present to me. There's a connection, a quiet communication between whatever I noticed and me. It conveys a word or thought to me simply because I notice it. When I look at a piece of art, I sometimes ask myself what word or thought comes to mind as I study the painting or collage or drawing. I'm trying to apply that same kind of noticing to other things. Like a house. A flower. A tree. At the moment, I'm looking at one of the elm trees in my back yard. What is it "telling" me? It speaks of steadiness. Stay steady, it says. The winds may blow, but stay steady.

19

Just before the Covid-19 outbreak, I traveled with friends to VietNam and Cambodia. Among my beautiful memories are the hundreds of white phalaenopsis orchids that billowed out of a massive pot in the lobby of a hotel in VietNam and a similar one in the airport in Seoul. I grow the same kind of orchids in a terra cotta pot the size of a large coffee mug. My orchids grow on a single stem, but they are no less beautiful. The elegant arc of the stem holds ten white blooms lined shoulder to shoulder. Each bloom opens to a deep magenta center. What do they say to me? "Let quietness and beauty enrich the very center of your life."

20

In honor of my silver-gray cat:
Pad,
pause,
purr,
sneak,
stalk, slipper-soft
peek,
peer,
pounce.

– kh –

21

I've just seen a photograph from inside the National Library of Austria, built in the 1700s. The entire library holds over seven million books. This picture shows a large space at least three stories high and open to the domed ceiling, which, along with the upper walls, is painted in a way that reminds me of what I might see in the Sistine Chapel in Rome. Three round windows grace these upper walls. They look more than tall enough for me to stand up in. The floor is designed in tan and brownish red marble that's polished to reflect the gleam from the warm yellow lights on the walls. In the center of the floor is a Roman-looking statue on a tall pedestal. But it's the walls that hold the treasure: books. Two floors of books in reddish-wood shelves surround the sides of this open room, the lower marble-floored area, and the upper area lined with a narrow balcony. As I look at the picture, I can smell this book-scented room. I can hear the echo of my footsteps as I walk across the marble floor. I have never been there, but I have been there.

22

It's not what you look at that matters,
it's what you see.

– Henry David Thoreau –

In the course of a day, I look at a million things. What I see—that's a much lower number.

23

Yesterday, I was driving through an unfamiliar complex of office buildings, and I turned a corner to find a pond in a field that looked as if it was planted with geese. They were standing tall and still, their long black necks stretched up at attention. Maybe they were watching the weather, testing the wind, ready to fly when the signal came. I didn't take the time to stop and see. I, too, was watching the weather. I was "flying" home.

24

Four clear glass bulb vases stand in a line along one of the windowsills in my sunroom. Each holds a hyacinth bulb that sits just above the waist of the vase with a network of roots spreading out in water below. Pink, white, and blue blossoms once bunched together in fragrant columns on each stem, but they wilted some time ago. The leaves are still green, though, and the thread-thin roots seem quite happy to web out into the water. I hope they'll bloom again next year. When I think of them, I can almost smell their perfume. I think life might be that way. When we think back to times when we bloomed, we can almost catch the fragrance of those days. But we still have roots and a bit of greenery, so we have every hope that we'll bloom again and again.

25

I'm at a lodge on a ranch outside Nashville with friends old and new. We're here to celebrate a treasured friend's birthday. During the day, we swim and laugh and stroll beside the river. Late in the afternoon, billowy clouds with gray bellies move in, and we walk in a fresh breeze to a refurbished barn where we'll eat dinner. Shortly after we arrive, the wind picks up, the clouds darken, and we find ourselves sheltering in the barn from a torrential downpour. Rain spills in a waterfall over the open sides of the barn, but that only adds to our sense of adventure. Once the rain subsides, we eat, share memories, sing and dance, and toast our birthday friend. Then in the deep country darkness, I walk back to the lodge with a small group of friends, each of us lighting our way with our phones. The rain has brought us a chilly night, but we leave the windows open, and at bedtime, we snuggle under our blankets. One by one, our whispers drop away, and we fall asleep to the late-night whispers of nature herself.

26

Wonder is not
precisely knowing
and not precisely
knowing not.

– Emily Dickinson –

Some wonders are sudden and breathtaking like seeing a falling star. Some wonders are deeper and soul-stirring like holding the tiny hand of a newborn baby. Either way, we're filled with awe and unanswered—maybe even unanswerable—questions. And we wonder. Maybe it's wonder that powers the progress of the world. Maybe it's wonder that leads us higher, takes us deeper, sends us farther. I wonder how. I wonder who. I wonder when. I wonder what and what if. We wish for certainty, but maybe certainty is stagnation. Maybe it's uncertainty that propels us. Maybe it's wonder that keeps us alive.

27

I picked up a scrap of paper from the floor today, a tiny scrap, small as a shelled sunflower seed. It was the shape of a heart. I always pause when I find a heart somewhere unexpected—in petals or leaves, in the pattern of wood grain, in the shape of a shadow or a splash of light. Or, like today, a snippet of paper. I set this tiny paper heart on the darkened face of my phone and carried the phone like a tray upstairs to my desk. This scrap of heart, this snippet, is a reminder that love can be found in the quietest whispers, in the tiniest hand to hold, in a single touch or word, in the faintest beat of my heart.

28

My preschool grandchildren played at a neighborhood park today and spent a lot of time on the see-saws, learning to manage the ups and downs. I thought of life, learning to manage the ups and downs and sudden slants that send us high when we're low or low when we're high, in when we're out or out when we're in. Life is a see-saw, and I hope to ride its ups and downs with as much determination and joy as my grandkids have right now.

29

Being friends with artists is a glorious joy. My house is a gallery of their work. Deanie and Nadine are in my sunroom. Dave is in the dining room, Jenni in the living room. My bedroom holds Karen and Roberta, Robin and Doris and Jen. I am richly blessed by the creativity and the presence of these creative spirits, these lovely, artful friends.

30

I've decided that the word for my black-eyed Susans is "picturesque." Tall stems curve them left or right so that they come to pose in front of a background of white windflowers or rest among the magenta and yellow lantana or sway before the creeping Jenny. Three Susans stand in a thin, blue-glazed pottery bud vase that my older son and his family gave me. I think if these black-eyed Susans could, they would take selfies—see us posed here for you, a still life in real life, they would say. Yes, I see you. I see your splashes of golden joy.

31

A welcome rainstorm just passed through, drenching trees and sunburned grass and thirsty flowers, leaving the world in a soft, green glow. Branches are still dripping, and the air is hazy with heat. The stillness is striking. It's as if the backyard world has been caught in a freeze-frame, holding its breath, utterly, silently, majestically still. For the moment, like me.

JUNE

1

I have a theory. It's unprovable, but I think it's probably true: Animals were the world's first entertainment. I suspect that before internet and television, before radio and even books, way back at the beginning of time and for centuries after that, people did a lot of animal-watching. Monkeys swung like acrobats from tree to tree, squirrels scampered in spirals chasing each other up tree trunks, birds fluffed their feathers and sang and performed their fancy mating dances, goats leaped, cats chased their tails, dogs nosed into mud puddles and came up smiling. Maybe the converse is true as well. Maybe to animals, people were the original entertainment. Maybe we still are.

2

Someone posted the phrase "unsettled skies," and that thought has stayed with me today. It's exactly the description for the rainclouds that are rolling in— billows of dark gray, shifting and moody, swept along by a gusty wind. Makes me feel a bit unsettled myself.

3

    The Texas afternoon is bright and clear and stinging hot. I'm on vacation, and everyone is at the pool—my two sons, their wives, and their children. I'm content to lounge on a chair under a canopy of a broad crape myrtle. Now and then, pink ruffled blossoms drift down. I wonder what time I should start making dinner. I back-time it and settle on 5:00. Maybe. But it is not 5:00 now. I send thoughts of dinner drifting off like crape myrtle blooms in the breeze. This is my time off, and now is my moment to lie back under this leafy canopy, close my eyes, feel the breeze on my skin, and listen to playful splashes and the happy voices that I love most.

4

It's our last night at the lake.
The water is as blue as forever.
The distant hills rest
in dusky silhouette against
the wine-red sunset,
which deepens by the minute
into darkness.
The lake gently ripples,
its blue deepens,
and the lantern at the end of the dock

blinks on,
glowing white, tinted with yellow,
a steady point in the passing of time,
in the slosh of the lake on the shore,
in my resting heart.

– kh –

5

The first butterfly I've seen this year swept past the wildflowers today like white-winged snow drifting down from one of our billowing cumulus clouds. I thought the wildflowers would attract her, the coreopsis, coneflowers, and windflowers. But she swooped past each one, past the bees busy with black-eyed Susans, past the geraniums. She looked like she was on the way to somewhere important—like the White Rabbit in Alice in Wonderland. But maybe she doesn't know her destination. Maybe she's flying for the joy of it. Maybe she'll land only when she's completed a tour of the garden and waltzed with the breeze.

6

Uptail, the chipmunk scampers between a pot of dahlias yet to bloom and a pot of lily-of-the-valley with their white, bell-like blossoms. This chipmunk is no doubt the one my cat watches—and probably chases when she's outdoors. It lives with its partner in a tunnel under the front garden next door. I watch the pair from my kitchen window. It's the only time I see them together. Is only one brave enough to venture into known cat territory? This one knows I am careless with seeds when I refill the birdfeeder. The seed bag is large and unwieldy, and as I tip it up, a few seeds— or lots—spill overboard onto the deck. I leave them there. I enjoy seeing this brave little uptail chipmunk fill his pouched cheeks.

7

Late this afternoon as I washed my hands to begin preparing supper, I noticed a fine spider web on the outside of the window above the kitchen sink. It's draped in a swoop like a pulled-back curtain and is hair-thin, so fine that it's hardly noticeable when it's in shadow. But as the sun lowers, each thin strand turns iridescent. I feel protective of this gift. It's a prism all my own.

8

I find coneflowers fascinating. The red-orange kind are the first to emerge in my garden. They remind me of little circus tents unfolding. At first, they're a bit striped, because the lighter underside of the petals outline the bolder-colored upper side. But as the days go by, the petals stretch out and then down a bit, hiding their undersides and holding their large mounded centers up to the sun. They continue to fade day by day until they're a lighter orange like peach ice cream. Then they turn pale yellow. But the bees and butterflies are drawn to the dark, rounded, lightly scented, pincushion center of the bloom. To them, the petals are only welcome mats.

9

Today is my oldest grandson's birthday. He's nineteen. I blinked, and he grew up. Not so long ago, he was a baby. As I held him, my first grandchild, I saw something that only grandparents can see. In that baby, I saw the toddler, the first grader, the pre-teen, the adolescent, and the man he would become. I went through all those stages with his father, and now I saw all of them in this one tiny baby. It was one of those magical gifts that come with being a grandparent.

10

The talking stick doesn't really talk.
Long and smooth,

it's passed hand to hand
around our circle
as it has been passed
through the years,
hand to hand,
fist to fist,
clutched,
fingered,
held close,
a lifeline,
a reassurance,
a permission to remember,
an invitation to vulnerability,
visibility,
acceptance,
change.
The talking stick has heard stories
from bared hearts.
It's been entrusted with
fears,
dreams,
hopes.
The talking stick has heard it all.
The talking stick
doesn't really talk.
But, oh, if it did . . .

– kh –

11

My front yard is a carpet of clover with round clusters of white blossoms. Once in a while, I think about creeping through it to look for a four-leafed clover, although finding one out of a whole yard full would in itself be a stroke of good luck. Just having a yard of clover is pretty lucky, if you ask me. It's lovely to look at and perfectly soft and cool for bare feet to walk on. You just have to watch for bees. They think it's lovely too.

12

I stepped outdoors to enjoy the evening warmth after being in air-conditioning all day. As I admired my newly potted geraniums, I heard a chirpy squeal nearby. For a minute, I thought it might be my cat. It sounded strained the way she sounds when she's in trouble. But when I turned to look, there sat a gray-brown squirrel on the lowest limb of the crape myrtle about three feet away, clucking and chirping and squealing at an intruder—me. I've rarely been that close to a squirrel, so I stood as still as I could. I stared at her, and she stared at me with her shiny dark eyes. She chirred a warning. I didn't move. She skittered to the next branch up and hugged it to her silver-white belly. Her thin tail was as long as the rest of her body, and she waved the end of it like a starting flag at a Nascar race. But she kept the rest of her body still. She waited, clucking, squealing, and tail-waving. I waited silently. Then she returned to her lower perch, and I wondered if she would be brave enough to approach me and see what type of creature had so rudely invaded her territory. But then my cat trotted past, and the squirrel scampered. She may not know who I am, but she knows a cat when she sees one.

13

A family of finches has taken over the birdfeeder this morning. The feeder is a seed-filled cylinder with four perches at four openings, and the finches gather around it as if they own the place. A cardinal can send finches scattering. A blue jay can too. But there are no cardinals or blue jays here today, only a nuthatch, who holds back, waiting, perched on the crook of a garden stake a few feet away. He keeps his back turned, glancing at the finches now and then as if to say, "Don't mind me. I'm not after your seeds." At last, the finches fly off and the nuthatch darts over. In his usual upside-down position, he snatches a seed and then darts away with a tasty reward for his patience.

14

    This morning I heard a clear, pure warble, a liquid-like waterfall of melody coming from somewhere in the back yard. I peered out the window and studied the trees, trying to follow the birdsong. Finally, I saw the singer: a small brown wren. I turned back to the tasks of the day happier for having seen the little wren, for having heard her song. In the midst of all our world's crazy and horrible and dangerous and questionable events, nature just keeps blooming and fading and offering herself, usually as a quiet and steady backdrop to our lives, although sometimes nature is the main attraction, thundering, blustering, flaming, and flooding. No matter what we humans do, no matter how oblivious we are, nature finds a way to keep budding in cracks and crevices, nesting in rafters or ruins, shining and shading and singing and filling space in a beautiful way.

15

Windows. I love them. All kinds. Some of my favorites stretch from wall to wall on three sides of my sun room. Morning light streams in from the east, the glow of sunset drifts in from the west, and moonlight chases the shadows at night. When the weather is friendly, I open these windows and invite the breeze in and with it, birdsong and the sound of mowing and a neighbor's loud "hey!" thrown across the fence to the man next door. I like the view from inside looking out. There's the tall elm in the southwest corner of the yard, the birds that visit the feeder of sunflower seeds—gray titmouse, black-capped chickadee, crimson cardinals, and red-tinted house finches. The view is always new, because Nature is always orchestrating some new song, painting some new picture, producing some new real life movie that's constantly streaming. Windowflix. I have subscribed.

16

I discovered a firefly on a lampshade tonight. He probably came in when I let the cat in a while ago. I gently scoop him up, carry him in a soft, open fist to the back door, and step outside. Dozens of his companions are flickering in the twilight across the grass and under the pines. I toss him up and out. It feels like releasing a spark of magic.

17

Couples are out this evening walking around the block. They stroll, jog, power-walk, dog-walk; they're a familiar sight. Earlier in the day, I saw an unusual walker: a crow, black and sleek. He was strutting herky-jerky down the street as if out for a casual stroll. I watched him pass four yards, and then he took off in flight. Maybe he had grown tired of walking. I wonder if joggers, dog-walkers, and couples out for a stroll ever wish they could fly.

18

I retrieved a marble from under the rocking chair. It's a night-blue marble with a swirl of gold in it, one of the lost ones separated from its fellow marbles of green and red, cat's eyes and shooters. My grandchildren left this morning, the three-year-old with the spark of mischief in her eyes, the five-year-old with a hesitant, questioning look in his glance. Why do I clasp this marble, round and hard in my palm and pause for a moment before putting it away? Why do I feel a tightness in my throat and a burning of tears behind my eyelids? Maybe I'm realizing the vastness of the realm of time, the passing of it, that these children who tossed and lost the marble are now up and out and busy with something else. Perhaps I'm trying to hold a moment in that marble. Perhaps this tiny blue, gold-flecked sphere connects me to the memory of their invitation to play—busy, strong, intense, and in person—and the invitation is gone now; they are distant. Perhaps it's the yearning, the feel, the play, the richness of relationship, the hope, the knowledge that all things change, the realization that happiness and heartache live together. Perhaps it's the letting go, the understanding that this little girl, this young boy will go their own way and take their own journeys, which are just beginning while mine is ending. Who knew one blue marble could hold all this?

19

To rain or not to rain—that seems to be the question the skies are asking today. Castles of gray clouds cover the sun and darken the daylight, but the edges of the clouds are bright white. As they creep across the sky, they leave space between each other for the deep blue beyond to show through. To rain or not to rain—the clouds have no answer. I think it will be a spontaneous decision.

20

A goldfinch landed in the black-eyed Susans while I was eating lunch today. The bright little bird seemed to like one bloom in particular and perched there for a couple of minutes. He was almost the same color as the Susans. I tiptoed across the room to get my phone-camera, afraid he'd dart away at my movement. But when I returned, he was still busily pecking at the dark seed-center of the bloom. He looked up and around as I focused in, then went back to foraging. He took his time. And I took mine.

21

A Montessori catalogue came in the mail today. Sometimes I find birthday or holiday presents in it for my younger grandkids. Sometimes I find items that I want for myself. Like toaster tongs made of wood that you can use to get a stuck piece of toast out of the toaster. Or a nut cracker with a big screw that turns to crack a nut. Or a small porcelain pitcher or bowl that's just right for small young hands—or large older hands that like small pitchers and bowls. In this catalogue, there were glass bowls, and the description recommended sorting beans in them. It specifically mentioned that "the pleasing 'tink' of a transferred bean is its own reward." And this I know to be true.

It's singing in my memory. The 'tink' of a dried bean. The shoosh of pouring salt. The soft rattle of rice. Each is its own reward.

22

I've been thinking of something that A.A. Milne wrote in *The House at Pooh Corner*: "Poetry and Hums aren't things which you get, they're things which get you. And all you can do is to go where they can find you." I think of Poetry and Hums as the delights and inspirations that come to us as we pause, as we rest, as we notice the small daily gifts in the world around us. Poetry and Hums often meet me in the botanical gardens, at the art studio, in the lovely church I attend, and in my own yard. But the real "where" is the place in our hearts where we dream and the space in our souls where we're open to possibility. Helen Keller said, "The best and most beautiful things in the world cannot be seen or even touched. They must be felt with the heart." That's where Poetry and Hums can always find us.

23

The golden light from my neighbor's kitchen windows is reflecting in my back window. The glow is layered over the glass at the exact place where I see the broad trunk of a tree beyond in the yard. The reflected light on the windowpane overlays the tree so that it makes bright golden, rectangular windows high up on the tree trunk. It looks like something out of Peter Pan's Never-Never Land. In this midsummer twilight with fireflies flickering here and there, reflected light has created a fairy world, a fantasy of an evening.

24

"One of the hardest lessons we have to learn in this life, and one that many persons never learn, is to see the divine, the celestial, the pure, in the common, the near at hand—to see that heaven lies about us here in this world." – John Burroughs

Late afternoon eases into twilight, one of my favorite times of day. The daytime buzz of bugs shifts into the nighttime buzz. The raspy song of the cicada gives way to the more wiry-sounding insects and the melodic chirps of crickets until at last, in the dark, the cicadas hush and the crickets take the lead, joined by tree frogs and the occasional high, wavering call of a screech owl. Heaven lies about us here in this world.

25

I hadn't made pudding in ages, the homemade kind. But I had over two cups of milk left over from a visit with my older son and his family, which includes two preschoolers. The only thing I could think to cook that would use a lot of milk was pudding. So I brought out the pan and sugar and milk and cornstarch and unsweetened chocolate squares (because, of course, my pudding must be chocolate). And I began. Lots of stirring was involved. But I had time. The pudding thickened and bubbled and began smelling like the real thing. And I pulled my focus into the moment. Nothing past to worry about right then, nothing future—though there was plenty of both if I let myself go either direction—but peace is found in the present, in the now, which in that moment meant noticing a gently ticking clock, the soft purr of the air conditioner, a wren warbling outside, and pudding bubbling on the stove. "Look past your thoughts so you may drink the pure nectar of this moment," said Rumi. The pure nectar of this moment tastes like chocolate pudding.

26

I have been acquainted with the night.

– Robert Frost –

When my older son was a preschooler, he asked me to close the blinds at night "so the dark won't come in." Actually, when the lights are off indoors, outdoors often looks lighter. On the other hand, some nights do seem coal black outdoors. No moon. No ambient light. I've occasionally woken up from a deep dream into that kind of darkness and blinked my eyes, wondering for a moment where I am. Tonight is one of those dark nights. I peer out at it through my kitchen window and see the yellow street light winking at me. I know the winking doesn't come from the light but from the way leafy branches swish across it in the wind. All the same, I wink back. The cat stretches, eyes half-closed, and I head upstairs to bed, turning off lights as I go. I am acquainted with the night.

27

Gray-brown, rough-edged stones outline my neighbor's front garden in a casual, jumbled, they-just-happened-to-fall-here way. Between the stones are lots of gaps and overlaps where chipmunks hide. This morning, two chipmunks ran back and forth chasing each other, first sprinting, then stopping to stand as still as the border stones, blending in. Stop and start, dash and dart, scramble away from each other, then skitter back. I watched this morning exercise for a while. Then the chipmunks came face to face and seemed to work out some sort of agreement on their agenda for the day. One ran north, the other ran south, and the gray-brown stones were left to stand guard alone.

28

Do your work, then step back.
It's the only path to serenity.
– Lao Tzu –

Recently a friend and I shared a moment of frustration, amazed at how we wave away our worries intending to be rid of them, but they return creeping— or buzzing or zinging or whining—when we least want to deal with them. As my friend detailed one of her worries, I saw it as a balloon. "That's not your balloon," I told her. "Let it go."

I've since pictured each of us holding a bunch of helium balloons like a bouquet. But only a few of them are rightfully ours to hold. The rest belong to someone else, to situations we can't control or cure. If we let go of those and let them float away, we're left with the few that do belong to us. Then we do our work, step back, and one by one, let those balloons go too. "It's the only path to serenity."

29

It's nearing July 4, and it's apparent from all the buds on the crape myrtle, that it's going to celebrate with an explosion of blooms, pyramid-shaped panicles pointing in all directions, fragrant fireworks in pink. I planted this crape myrtle years ago, thinking it would be a plump, shrub-sized tree. It's now as high as the rooftop of our second-story house. I think that's how my life has worked. It has greatly outgrown my expectations.

30

One of the advantages of having a daughter-in-law who is an expert at quality control in the coffee business is getting to try a variety of really good coffees. I think part of the joy of coffee-tasting—or wine-tasting or cheese-tasting—simply comes from the wonder of trying something for the first time— tasting a new combination of flavors at a restaurant, hearing a new song, catching the scent of a new fragrance. Or maybe it's not something new, but something rare like seeing an eclipse or a falling star or a super moon rising. And maybe if we can see from the perspective of a child who pauses, touches, smells, hears, and looks at common things for the first time, then maybe, just maybe we can bring back the wonder and joy.

SUMMER

JULY

Clouds, white on gray and gray on white,
slide across the sun and dim the afternoon light.
Rain?
I'm hopeful.
A brisk breeze
sends a handful of dry brown leaves
twirling through the air.
Rain?
A grumble of thunder echoes.
Cloud bellies look full of
what we need so badly.
Rain.
A ray of sunlight streaks out
and beams hot across the thirsty grass.
We are flooded
with sunshine.
The rain has gone
elsewhere.

– kh –

2

The first rain droplets tap the window, and I gaze out skeptically. Is this rain? Truly? Or is this just a tease? In answer, the clouds let loose a soaking shower, a steady straight rain in strands of silver, puddling on the shingles next door, veiling distant trees, slaking the thirst of grass and tree, hedge and flower, birds and chipmunks. And me. I lie back and rest with the click of raindrops on the windowpanes and the roll of thunder, a contented grumble, from the throat of the sky.

3

. . . feel the stars and the infinite
high and clear above you.
Then life seems
almost enchanted after all.

– Vincent Van Gogh –

The night sky holds a fingernail of a moon, a waxing crescent. The sharp hook at the bottom of the crescent is periodically blurred by clouds drifting across it. I think of Van Gogh's "Starry Night," the way his crescent moon and stars seem to glow, rippling out into the swirls of his sky. I gaze up into this real-world, crescent-moon night, up into the infinite high that holds stars and planets and galaxies. It's a Van Gogh sky, and tonight, it seems enchanted.

4

A preschool friend of my grandson had a birthday party over the weekend. Her party favors were plastic bracelets embedded with different colors of lights that flash when they're turned on. So, of course, when my grandson came over today, he wanted to turn off all the lights so he could show me the twinkling colors. There was just one problem: the bright, sunny day. Even with the lights off, it wasn't dark. But not to worry. He knows where to find the dark. He led me into the basement, and we watched the lights flash to his heart's content. It made for a magical morning.

5

I miss my wristwatch. The band broke. I wonder if I can do without it. People often rely on their phones now to tell the time, and I do have a phone. It occurs to me that my grandson who is in kindergarten will probably not be taught to tell time on a clock with hands. I mention it to him, try to help him decode the mystery of the hour hand, the minute hand, the quick little tappy second hand and its tick-tock that now seems almost as old as . . . well, time. I try to make it a game, but it's not a game he wants to play. At least not now. He is digital. His minutes slip silently past, glowing from a microwave or an oven timer or the face of a phone. No figuring it out; it's just there, a bold declaration of "this is now." Of course, step away for a few moments and now will have slid along silently into then where it stays forevermore in that vast collection of minutes gone by. There's always a new now. How much time has passed as I've been writing this? I automatically glance at my wrist and shrug. I miss my watch.

6

The morning was unusually quiet. No birds ate at the feeder, no birds pecked around in the grass, no birds perched in the nearby trees. There were no squirrels or chipmunks either. That usually signals the presence of a hawk or falcon, so I looked up and, yes, there was a visitor soaring the sky above. A hawk slowly glided in a circle that encompassed our yard as well as our neighbors'. The thing about quiet is that it is not necessarily peaceful. This quiet was actually full of tension. It was only after the hawk flew away that real peace returned and birds came back to the feeder. Peace was full of birdsong.

7

I have seen the softness and beauty of the summer
clouds
floating feathery overhead,
enjoying, as it seemed,
their height and privilege of motion.

– Ralph Waldo Emerson –

Clouds that seem to be lying on "a flat, invisible floor of air" actually are. Gavin Pretor-Pinney, founder of the Cloud Appreciation Society and author of the book *A Cloud a Day*, says that this invisible floor "marks the condensation level. This is the height at which air, rising off the sun-warmed ground as a thermal, cools enough for its moisture to change from gas to liquid droplets." He calls the cumulus cloud that forms there "a snoozing beast of moisture." As Emerson would say, it's enjoying its height and privilege of motion.

8

Quiet,
to me as a young girl,
was a blue room,
a closed door,

a notebook and a novel.
Quiet was a pillow and blankets.
Quiet was my thoughts,
ideas and questions—
how?
why?
what-if?
Quiet was not knowing
about life outside this
silent, cozy den,
wanting to know but
not wanting to know.
Quiet was not knowing
who I was
or was becoming.

– kh –

9

I recently received a card in the mail from a friend
I hadn't heard from in a long time. The front of the
card showed a landscape of gray mountains under a
sky layered with lavender and blue. I set the card
beside my desk, and when I glanced at it later, I
realized that I had set it there with the scene upside
down. The sky was now at the bottom and looked like
a lavender and blue mountain range, and the
mountains looked like a dark gray sky. The whole

picture was an upside-down echo of the right-side-up view. I began to think of the interesting ways nature echoes herself in shape, line, color, and even sound. A butterfly can look like the petals of a flower—or petals can look like butterflies. Wind rushing through trees sounds like waves breaking on a shore—and waves sound like wind in the trees. Around and around nature goes reflecting herself, painting, singing, sculpting, and dancing in echoes.

10

Inebriate of air am I—
And debauchee of dew;
Reeling through endless summer days,
From inns of molten blue.

– Emily Dickinson –

Molten blue. That's how the sky looks on this sultry, cloudless day. And it's how I begin to feel if I stand outside for very long—molten.

11

The goldfinch is back this morning, and he has brought a friend. He perches on a dried stalk of bamboo that my grandson stationed on the platform at the top of the slide. The second goldfinch is foraging among the sunflowers, which have lost their bright petals. The sunflowers' round, brown faces bow toward the ground as if they are ashamed to have lost their sunny, showy skirts. But they have something more now. They have seeds—and the bright company of goldfinches.

12

To fear is one thing.
To let fear grab you by the tail and swing you around is another.

– Katherine Paterson, *Jacob Have I Loved* –

Peace. Inhale. Exhale. We hear lies and deceit but refuse to let them lodge in our souls. Instead, we counter them with integrity and breathe out to the world what is true. We see the ignoble and dishonorable raise its head, but we refuse to embrace it. Instead, we counter it with what's honorable and breathe out to the world what's noble. We see what's tainted with wrong, distill it, and exhale what's right. We see what's sloppy or mediocre, let it evaporate, and breathe out what's excellent. We see what's shameful but refuse to give it a home in our hearts. Instead, we give back what's worthy of praise. We refuse to let fear swing us around by the tail. We inhale, we exhale. We breathe peace.

13

This evening's night chorus
features a solo
singing repeated triplets
in a raspy, buzzing voice.
Backup singers hold long notes,
high and thin
growing loud in a smooth crescendo,
subsiding to a softer hum.
Loud again,
soft again,
swell and repeat.
It's the insects' joyful tribute
to summer.

– kh –

14

Sometimes we see a cloud that's dragonish;
A vapour sometime like a bear or lion,
A towered citadel, a pendant rock
A forked mountain, or blue promontory
With trees upon't, that nod unto the world
And mock our eyes with air.

– Shakespeare –

Today's clouds look airbrushed. They're drifting so
low in the sky, it's as if they haven't decided if they're
going to be fog or if they're going to float up to gather
themselves into billows of cumulus. Right now,
they're stretched out like material that the sky sculptor
might scoop up and form into mountains or bears or
lions—or dragons.

15

It has been a week since we've seen even a drop
of rain, and the temperatures are hitting 100°. So
when rain clouds blew in today, I was hopeful.
Unfortunately, they took a path south of us. Dahlia
leaves droop by noon, the basil sags, and I have to
water daily. I wonder . . . is this how drought starts, at
first just a dry spell in the background of our day-to-

day tasks that we assume will be broken any day now—until one day we realize we're in the middle of it? Is that how war starts? Can that possibly be the way peace starts?

16

It's a balancing act for the small downy woodpecker. She has bright eyes and a gray head, and right now, she's upside down clinging to a strand of wire crossing the bottom of the suet feeder. She's belly up with her black tail curved up for balance. It's a valiant see-saw effort to stabilize, but I know she won't get her meal until she abandons her upside-down perch for the wider side of the suet cage. That's where she can get in, and eventually she figures it out. She's a persistent little thing and doesn't know I'm watching on the other side of the window, applauding her success.

17

A bee is snooping around the snowdrop windflowers. Each small blossom looks like a delicate, white snow angel. The bee chooses one and nuzzles into the bloom's pale pink center. Both bee and blossom are as light as feathers. Even so, the whole stem lowers with the bee's weight. When the bee's visit is done, she flits away, leaving the stem bobbing as if these angel blossoms are themselves taking flight.

18

A firefly landed on a windowpane this afternoon and rested there in full sun. I almost didn't recognize it as a firefly, because I think of fireflies as night bugs. In broad daylight, it looked quite ordinary, like just another insect blending in with the hundreds, thousands, millions of buzzing, droning, flitting, fluttering, crawling, climbing insects. Until dark. Then fireflies are the ones who rise up, tiny flames flickering on and off and on again, an enchanting wonder of the night.

19

Two pink coneflowers have bloomed in the middle of my planter of black-eyed Susans, and while the stems of the Susans arch and bow, the coneflowers stand tall like big sisters supervising their bright, dancing siblings. One of the coneflowers has a bright orange, prickly puffed center. The other has a center tipped in yellow. Their petals curve down like paneled skirts. A bee seems quite happy to have found these little ladies. And so am I.

20

The marigolds that I planted in a long, raised flower box are fast growers, increasing in size every day. When I checked on their progress this morning, I found that they'd become a miniature forest for an ant or a ladybug or a fairy. I bent down to survey this marigold forest from a bug's-eye view. I felt like a giant peering through a grove that was rather tropical looking with trunks of red-brown and leafy tops of wide-spread fronds. I had planted them in two rows, so a miniature path passes between the plants, making the whole scene look not so much like a forest as a well-planned orchard or a tree-lined road leading to an estate. And I almost wish that fairies were real.

21

When the great depression hit in 1929, my grandad was a young man with a wife and a baby (my dad) to support, so he traveled around the South "feeling the country out, you know—for a job," he said. For a while, he loaded trucks by hand. Then he shoveled gravel, earning a dollar and a half a day. The family was poor, but they got by. As the years passed, Grandad worked hard at whatever he could find to do. Eventually he became a successful businessman and rancher. But along the way, he had his share of failures. He bought a hotel. It failed spectacularly. He bought a dairy farm. It didn't work out. He started raising sheep. No go. But Grandad always shook it off and moved on, saying, "Well, I learned what not to do," which in his view was just as valuable as learning what to do. Like they say out West, "When your horse dies, it's time to get off."

22

The sea's drawing tide flows and ebbs,
rushes and splashes,
lifelike,
now overwhelming and frightening,
now gentle and soothing,
now crashing, rushing, spewing, roaring,
never denied its power, its fullness,
but then gently foaming onto the shore.
The tide pools it leaves behind—
holding tiny crabs and brittle stars,
sand dollars and loops of kelp—
hint at its life,
the wholeness, the quietness
of diving under.
Who first dared to cross
the all-things-encompassing fullness of sea,
the washing, foaming swash of waves?
The journey had to be frightening,
daunting.

But so it is with the sea.
The distant horizon where water meets sky
holds a magnetic pull
that leads
to another shore.

– kh –

23

The weeks stood still in summer.

– Rainer Maria Rilke –

Here in Tennessee, summer is like a sauna, hot and steamy. This thick, heavy heat makes me feel like the whole world must have come to a standstill. Chilly weather energizes me—or maybe it inspires me to move briskly just to keep warm. But even my fastest movements midsummer feel like a slog through a swamp—a bloom-bountiful, leaf-beautiful swamp, but a swamp nonetheless. So here's to our sluggish, stand-still weather. Cheers to our glorious, sultry swamp!

24

I bought a pot of lantana. I've never grown them before, but our neighborhood grocery had pots of them on sale, so of course, I bought one. The fascinating thing about lantana is its varicolored blooms. Each is about the size of a silver-dollar and is made of rounded petals arranged in circular rows. On my plant, the first few outer rows are pink, and the next several inner rows are yellow. I'm sure a botanist could explain why this is, and no doubt, I could do a search to discover the answer myself. But then, not every curiosity needs to be explained. For the time being, I've decided to be content with the mystery and wonder of lantanas.

25

Now air is hushed, save where the weak-eyed bat,
With short shrill shriek flits by on leathern wing.

– William Collins –

The fish and reptile house at the zoo is dim inside. I went with my son and his family. We leaned closed to the glass of the exhibits as we studied snakes and lizards, beetles and fish. And bats. The small brown bats were quite close, some eating fruit, others asleep or resting, hanging upside down swaddled with their leathery wings. Soft leather. Supple. Veined. I would have loved to touch a bat's wings if I could have. They're quite the contrast to the long, feathery pink wings of the flamingoes we'd seen earlier. Bat wings, bird wings, bee wings, wasp wings. Butterflies, cicadas, fireflies, dragonflies, moths—dusty wings, thick wings, transparent wings. There must be a title for someone who specializes in the study of all the varieties of nature's wings. I think I might have enjoyed that career. At my age, a career is getting to be a thing of the past. But a wing-lover—I can be one of those.

26

My chorus line of white, magenta-throated orchids, my ballet-dancer blooms, has begun to thin. One by one they've let go of their stem until there are only two left now. I gently pick up my fallen dancers in their white skirts. They're extra soft now as they fade. I take them to my art studio, wondering if I can place them in a collage. Will they take the medium I'll have to brush over them? Can I keep them forever dancing?

27

As a word-lover, I often search back into history to find out how a word came to be. Word origins are always interesting to me, but sometimes they're ho-hum interesting, and sometimes they're wow interesting. Calm is kind of a wow. It can be traced back to the Latin cauma, which means "summer heat," with the "l" perhaps coming from calere, "to be hot." But calm doesn't mean "hot" now. Why not? The reason is logical. Before there was air conditioning (which is most of history), the hottest part of a summer day became a time out, a siesta to calm both body and mind. And there it is. Calm grew out of "hot" and became "a state of tranquility." Now, we don't have to be hot to take a time out and become calm; we can take a time out and be calm whatever the weather.

28

All morning, I've been watching a large, red-bellied woodpecker. He's snatching sunflower seeds from the birdfeeder, where he shares space with black capped chickadees and a titmouse, one of those lovely, gray, dark-eyed birds with a small crest on its head. The woodpecker shares by necessity, I think. He's too large to cling onto the feeder for long. When he lands on the perch, his head nearly reaches the top of the tube of seeds. He looks around (out of caution or just showing off, I don't know), then he scoots down as far as he can, dips into the opening, quickly snatches a seed, and flies off. The other birds flit back to get their share. I wonder if they see him as an intruder or a clown or just a big friend.

29

Rain slams down,
puddling, pooling,
blowing across rooftops in showery sheets,
bowing the bamboo with streaming wet ribbons.
The deluge comes in a rush,
a shush,
a whispery roar,
hitting the windows with prickly taps,
drumming the roof in a frenzied beat.
The thunderheads
are releasing their burden,
pouring their gift,
breaking the tension
of a hot, humid,
sultry
afternoon.

– kh –

30

I'm pressing my fallen orchid blooms, putting them
between two layers of waxed paper with two thick,
heavy encyclopedia books on top, volumes M and N-
O. Remember encyclopedias? Mine are ancient now,
but I still search them once in a while. Is it easier to

do an internet search? Maybe. But occasionally I like thumbing through these old hard copies. Today I'm glad to have them handy for a flower press.

31

If you've never been to the Hoh Rainforest, add it to your bucket list. Hiking its trails is like stepping into a fantasy world. It's a damp, mossy, green place. And it's a habitat for banana slugs. My family went when my boys were young. We took a hike guided by a park ranger. She showed us a banana slug, which, true to its name, is yellow and about the size of one of those small bananas that I sometimes see at the grocery store. The ranger held one of these slugs across her palm and told us that it secretes a slime that has an anesthetizing effect. She asked if anyone wanted to lick it. My older son did—and he did. With no ill effects. Except a temporarily anesthetized tongue. It's an interesting world.

August

1

One of the two feisty hummingbirds that fight over my feeder has chosen this morning to perch on the topmost, outermost twig of the crape myrtle. Usually he perches lower and deeper where he's hidden among the leaves. Since he's the same color as the leaves, he's camouflaged there, and at certain angles, I can't see him at all. But now on the top twig, he's in full view, silhouetted against the sky. He's so light that he barely bends the twig he's sitting on. In spite of his diminutive size, he looks as if he's the king surveying his kingdom, this wild back yard. He doesn't stay long, though. Maybe he's satisfied that all's well. Most likely, though, his sparring partner has left the feeder, and it's now his turn to feast.

2

My surprise lilies surprised me again. All the other lilies in my front garden took their turns blooming earlier in the summer, the orange first and then the yellow. All of them wilted weeks ago; their petals fell, and their stems dried into tan, crisp sticks. I looked for the surprise lilies then, but they didn't appear. And they didn't appear. And they didn't appear. And just when I began to think they had died out—surprise! Not only do they look as healthy as ever, but there are more than there were last year. Bouquet after bouquet after bouquet of pink, perfumed, trumpet-shaped lilies line the garden, each bouquet perched atop a leafless stalk. These lilies are a favorite, and I can truly say that they've earned their name.

3

When the mockingbird takes off, it flashes its white wing patches. A flicker reveals the yellow under its wings and tail as it flaps away. Today I watched a hummingbird hover. His wings were a blur, but his back was to me and his tail feathers were spread, so I got to see the three white patches on each side of his tail. I'm not officially a birdwatcher, but I do watch birds—at least enough to know that sometimes they're most beautiful when they fly.

4

There's something about a smooth surface that gives me a serene, restful feeling, a sense that all's well. Maybe it's a bit like fingering worry beads. When I get in bed at night, I often run my hand over the soft, smooth sheet. It's comforting, calming. My mug of coffee in the morning is round and smooth.

My favorite foods tend to be creamy like Greek yogurt or pudding or milk shake or ice cream or the now-forbidden dough of any kind. I suspect that it's good for me to know this about myself, although I'm all for experiencing a wide variety of textures, for the world is diverse, delightfully so. But for calm and comfort, I can't ask for anything better than smooth.

5

Yesterday, I spent the day at my younger son's house. He and his family have three dogs. I have a cat. Now there are lots of differences between dogs and cats, but yesterday I saw a difference I'd never noticed before. When dogs wag their tails, it's a non-stop wiggle. When cats "wag" their tails, it's a twitch. Then a long pause. Then another twitch. Or faster: whip-whip-pause-whip-whip-pause. For cats, even exuberance is subdued. Dogs are a definite here-I-am, here-I-am! Cats are a moody maybe.

6

My older son and his Japanese wife lived for almost six years in Japan, where they had two children, who are now six and three. They had never seen fireflies until they visited us in June. On many evenings, as twilight deepened into darkness, they would walk around our block on a firefly safari. And it was as if the fireflies put on a show just for them. Fireflies winked and blinked, rose from the grass like tiny flames, and twinkled high in the trees like fairy lights. They rested in gentle little hands and lit up like magic. The fireflies are long gone now. So are my son and his family, who have moved to California. Maybe they'll visit again next year when the fireflies return.

7

There are buds on my marigolds. I didn't notice them this morning. I didn't even pause to look, because I was focused on where I was heading: to spend the day with my grandson. Being with my grandson is a good thing, I know, a priority. So not pausing was not a big loss. I noticed the marigold buds when I returned home and watered my plants. They were a nice surprise after a busy day. But it made me realize that our usual paths can become so familiar that we don't notice our surroundings. We can wander through life with our minds traveling back to yesterday or forward to tomorrow or down into a screen, and we miss the patterns of petals on flowers and veins on leaves and seeds on grasses and anthills and vapor trails and puddles and roly-poly bugs. As photographer David Bailey said, "[I]t takes a lot of looking before you learn to see the ordinary."

8

Sometimes I catch a glimpse of something yellow streaking past a window that looks out on my deck. It's the goldfinch, who has taken to visiting regularly now. I'm sure his partner is around here somewhere. In years past, I've rarely seen goldfinches in my yard. In warm weather, one or two might stop by for a short sip from the birdbath. But these two keep returning. I think maybe they're going to stay for a while. I hope so. They are a bright hello.

9

Rain fell in large plops this afternoon, pelting the thirsty plants and dry ground. It was one of those pop-up summer storms. I've heard them called popcorn storms, presumably named after the cumulus clouds that look like giant popcorn in the sky. Thunder grumbled around for several minutes before the rain actually fell. Even then, it rained for only five minutes. But it was enough to wake the cat, who wanted to go out as soon as the rain stopped. When I opened the door to let her out, I had to pause to feel the heavy, humid air and inhale the scent of rain and wet soil, a rich smell. I breathed deeply of it as the cat prowled around the raindrop-spangled plants. Then the thunder cracked, and the cat darted inside. I scanned the sky. The sun was slipping in and out of cloud cover as a shower began. This could be a day for rainbows.

10

Night came down, and enfolded the earth
in her dusky wings.

– Virgil –

The hour is late, the sky is dark, the house is tired and quiet. The cat is curled in a chair asleep, the picture of total relaxation. Except once in a while, her paw twitches as if she's snatching something. It's a lazy snatch, the kind that catches a dream.

11

Yesterday, a red-tailed hawk at least eight inches tall perched on the top rail of the fence near our sunroom windows. His eight inches did not include his dark tail tipped in white, which extended down over the fence rail for balance. This hawk had a mottled breast of rust and white feathers, a dark head, and bright yellow feet. The bird book I grabbed showed that he was an immature red tail. I was surprised that he stayed so long, at least five minutes, maybe more. So I stayed too, just out of sight, watching him.

All was quiet. Awe-fully quiet. The bird feeder was nearby, but my wise little birds were in hiding. A squirrel on top of the swing set was frozen in a crouch, focused on the hawk, who ruffled his dark shoulders and scratched himself. After a long look around, he shot up at a steep angle northward. I went outside to check the mailbox and heard a deep rumble of thunder. I imagined the hawk piercing the clouds at that moment. The King of Thunder.

12

Last night I read about sunsets, the kind with big, billowy clouds that glow red and orange and gold. As it happens, in our atmosphere, blue light disperses better than red light, so as the sun lowers, its rays strike the clouds sideways. Cloud expert Gavin Pretor-Pinney says in his book *A Cloud a Day*, the "cool blueish rays are teased out." That leaves the gold and red rays to reach our clouds and give us warm sunset colors.

13

The crape myrtle bark, a dull light brown, has begun peeling as it does every year. Underneath is a mahogany color, a brown-orange that shows up in long, smooth streaks as its light brown outer bark sheds. It's not scaly like the dogwood or lumpy bumpy like the hackberry or furrowed like the pines. As the top layer curls away and sheds, it's stripped and striped and smoothly new. "Shed the old," it says. "Make way for the new."

14

As I was reading about interesting words and their backstories, I came across August. This month was named for the first emperor of the Roman Empire, whose real name was Caius Octavianus. He was the nephew of the famous Julius Caesar, who secretly adopted him. When Julius Caesar died, he willed everything to Caius. Many years later, when Caius became the ruler of the Roman Empire, he was given the title Augustus, which meant "imperial majesty." Since the fifth month of the year had been named Julius after his uncle, the sixth month became known as Augustus—our August. But Augustus (the month) was one day shorter than the month of Julius, and that wouldn't do. So those in charge of such things took one day from February and added it to August. Which short-changed February, but maybe it kept the peace.

15

    My lovely, longtime neighbors are moving. Our kids grew up together, and I guess I thought they'd be next door neighbors forever. But now there's a For Sale sign in their front yard, and I've become a bit weepy. This morning, a variety of unfamiliar voices is drifting from beyond the bamboo between our driveways. Strangers are touring the house and yard. I wonder which of these strangers will become neighbors. I also wonder if they're taking a peek at my garden, which needs a good weeding. Ah, well, I think. Full disclosure. Transparency and all that. I might as well let them see what they're likely to see if they move in, the fruits of a haphazard gardener. The house next door may change. I doubt if I ever will.

16

I spied a spider web today on my back deck. It was a wide one, stretching from a side table to the wall of the house. A dozen or so small, brown crape myrtle leaves were caught in this net of thread-thin filaments, which was invisible until the sun glanced at it at just the right angle. In the shade, the leaves appeared to be suspended in the air mid-tumble in a freeze-frame montage of late summer. "Look," they seem to say. "We are the first to fall, but we are not the last." I'm going to watch this web over the next few weeks to see just how many leaves it can hold.

17

When I was in elementary school, I loved looking at pictures in geography and earth science books, seeing places and people and animals and plants that I'd never seen before. I love it. I follow a site that posts pictures of unusual birds. I just saw a picture of a pheasant with feathers arranged like fish scales, white on his head and neck, iridescent green on his breast, and vivid blue on his back. Each feather, no matter its color, is outlined in black. Then there's the brilliant blue red-legged honeycreeper, who looks like he's wearing a black jacket. And the bright green magpie with red feet, red eyes, and a red beak. I could go on and on. Nature does. And that's just birds. Fish, insects, flowers—nature is extravagant. Extravagantly creative, extravagantly generous.

18

My coffee cup smiles at me as I look at it from where I sit at the breakfast table. The circle of its top is angled back from this view so that I'm looking over the rim, and the side nearest me is curved like a smile. It's the same with my water glass, mugs, bowls, even vases. The rim nearest me is always in a smile. If I rotate the cup or bowl, the rim nearest me is still a smile. Always the smiles are toward me. But the beauty of it is that if you sit on the other side of my cup or if you share my bowl or if we sit with a vase of flowers between us, it smiles at you, too.

19

My new dahlias are finally starting to bloom. I planted six of them and had no idea what color each of them would be, so I've been eagerly waiting for them to open. The blooms start as smooth, round green buttons of buds that swell day by day. For weeks, I've thought, today they'll open. But no. The next day, I look again. Today, I think. But no. They plumped out like tomatillos. Then, when they looked as if they might burst, they unfolded. The first bloomed salmon pink. The second bloomed a yummy vanilla color. There are still four plants to go. They have big, beautiful green buds. Maybe today.

20

The white butterfly that I saw earlier in the summer was back today. Or maybe it was one of her kin. She landed on the white windflowers and sat there riding the thin stems in the breeze. She looked exactly like one of the blooms. Nature's white on white.

21

I think my mother kept every greeting card that was ever sent to her. After she died, my sisters and I were cleaning out her laundry room and found two large, deep drawers stuffed with cards. I keep cards for a while, but unless the card is very special, I end up throwing it away. I don't remember most of them. But one card I got years ago contained a message I've never forgotten: "Life is always a size too big. You have to grow into it." I was maybe in my forties when I got that card. I'm now into my seventies. And life? It's still too big, and I'm still trying to grow into it.

22

A shower of dry leaves drifted down from the hackberry this morning, and this afternoon, a rainstorm blew in, leaving behind a breeze that carried a hint of coolness, a foreshadowing of autumn. Again, the seasons are teasing each other as a sweltering summer tries to hang on and a crisp autumn tries to elbow in and take over. Summer will win for a while, but in the end, autumn will nudge her offstage. And we who are craving cooler weather will breathe a sigh of relief.

23

The bees are busy today, making a buffet of the prickly pincushion centers of coneflowers, dipping into the dainty windflowers, snooping around the black-eyed Susans. I was going to snip some fresh blooms for my blue bud vase, but I didn't have the heart to disturb the bees or take their lunch away. So I just watched them flit and feast. The bud vase can wait.

24

The cardinals are the first birds to venture out as this morning's rain slows and softens. The bright red

male sits high on the crook of the hook where the
feeder hangs. As he keeps watch, the female, a
brownish red, snatches seeds. But I hear other birds
who are perhaps thinking of coming out now that the
rain has stopped. The wren is clearest of all with her
cheery chortling, a thank-you to the rain. Or maybe
she's calling for the cardinals to "leave some for me."

25

Along the sidewalk this morning, I saw several
fallen leaves, mostly brown or yellow-brown. I briefly
noticed them and moved on, thinking about autumn
to come. Then another fallen leaf caught my eye. It
was red-orange dappled in yellow-green with yellow
veins. I picked it up by its coffee-colored stem and
took it home with me. It's beside me now on my desk.
It's still summer-hot outside, but I've brought a bit of
autumn indoors.

26

On social media today, the video of a gunman was
making the rounds. I was not looking for it. It found
me, this killer stalking into a building. I knew how the
story ended, at least for that day, and I scrolled on.
The next post was a video of a peacock with a brilliant
blue body. He was spreading his tail like an enormous

fan of bright green feathers with blue "eye" dots to match his body. It struck me that those two videos juxtaposed are a symbol of our lives, horror and beauty side by side. They don't balance out. I don't let them. I watch the peacock and his fascinating tail-fan over and over again. I know that the ugly and evil exists, but I purpose to hold beauty and goodness in my thoughts and in my heart. I purpose to live it and leave it shimmering in my tracks.

27

This is the time of year that could well be called The Drift for a couple of reasons. For one, as each day passes, a few more leaves let go of the trees and drift to the ground. But also, summer is drifting toward fall like a rowboat set loose without paddles, drifting lazily down a gentle river. When will we get there? Who knows? The question is, are we noticing? Are we paying attention to the journey, the slow drift, the sights and sounds, the scents and flavors and textures that we pass along the way?

28

It's hosta season. Their large bouquets of leaves have been content to sit on the ground for weeks, soaking up the summer sun until they were ready to send up tall, thin stems and line them with buds. Last week, they decided it was time. They filled out with light purple buds veined in darker purple. The petals of the buds are folded up, cupping their centers protectively the way my grandson's hands cup a newfound treasure to hide and protect it. This week, the buds began to open. Each bloom has six purple petals pointed at the tips. Deep inside where the petals connect to each other, they're white. From that inner sanctum, one pure white pistil and six white filaments rise taller than the petals and curve gently down like a swan's neck. At the end of each filament is a tiny, elongated, dark purple anther with two thin, tan-gold stripes on their faces. I am amazed. There is nothing careless here. It doesn't matter to this hosta, this precise, meticulous beauty, whether or not I pause here to look closely. Hostas will keep budding and blooming and being beautiful, because that's who they are. No, it doesn't matter to the hosta if I notice it or not. But it does matter to me.

29

O to be a dragon,
a symbol of the power of Heaven—of silkworm
size or immense; at times invisible.
Felicitous phenomenon!

– Marianne Moore –

I just saw a dragonfly on my back deck, hovering over the water in the bowl I keep out for my cat. She dipped and rose like a little side-winged helicopter. I rarely see a dragonfly in my yard, and she didn't stay long—less than a minute. I guess she was satisfied and had to be on her way. But she has stayed in my mind, this silkworm-size dragon, this felicitous phenomenon.

30

The mandevilla vine has overgrown its trellis. One arm of the vine has angled out as if it's reaching for something solid that isn't there. It has remained in that reaching position for a week, and today, that vine-arm blossomed with two white, gold-throated blooms. It looks like it's content to stop reaching and will live outstretched now, offering its cups of gold to the world. It occurs to me that every plant can offer only what it has and what it is. Basil offers only basil. The dahlia offers only dahlias. The marigold offers only marigolds. That's all they have. That's all they are. And it's enough. That's what my garden tells me this morning. You can only offer what you have and what you are. And that's enough.

31

A leaf quivers on a branch and my heart trembles.
The wind stirs the leaves and beauty stirs my heart.

– Rumi –

A light summer shower came up suddenly, and I ran to the back door to see if the cat was scrambling to get in out of the rain. I opened the door so she would hear it if she had sheltered nearby, so she would know there was a way to get inside. I guess she was already in, because she didn't show up. What came in was the lovely scent of summer rain. I stepped outside under the eaves and stood there just out of the reach of the shower. A blue jay called from a tree on my right, answered by another jay from a tree to my left. A bee flitted around the mint blossoms. Raindrops gently tapped on the deck and flicked the leaves of the marigolds, making them shiver. But the shower stopped as suddenly as it started. I took one more deep breath of the rain-scented air. How can my heart hold any more beauty? I am full. For today, I am full.

SEPTEMBER

1

Blueberries,
berry blue,
you are a favorite of mine.
Roundly plump,
juicy bites,
you are all sweetness and tang.
I've seen you on bushes,
row after row,
covered with netting
to keep birds away,
for blueberries,
berry blue,
you are a favorite
of birds too.

– kh –

2

An elegant, sleek mockingbird is trying to get into the suet feeder. He flutters and shifts and tries to poke through the wire cage, which has openings just the right size for smaller birds. He's hopeful but a bit too large. Finally, he flaps up to the solid top of the cage and sits for a few seconds, looking around—disappointed, I think. I wish he could get in, but if the openings were larger, the squirrels would have a feast, and the small birds would be left with nothing. After the mockingbird flies off, a little flicker slips into the suet feeder. It's a perfect fit. He's pecking at his breakfast. For now, it's all his.

3

Faith is the soul riding at anchor.

– Josh Billings –

I don't often go out in a boat, but I have rafted rapids. I've cruised the inner passage in Alaska. I've ridden in a gondola in Venice. And I've taken the night boat from Guangzhou, China, to Hong Kong. But while I enjoy the adventure of traveling by boat, I find it comforting to ride at anchor, resting, gently rocked by the water. So the soul riding at anchor is a comforting thought. As far as faith goes, I see it as our spiritual disposition, the slant of our hearts toward what we value most in life. Faith holds us, supports us, keeps us on course and steady. It's our souls deeply anchored.

4

The leaves of the hackberries and elms have taken on a yellowish hue. The maple across the street is beginning to blush with a faint hint of red. And this morning, I noticed the first pure yellow leaf on the tulip poplar in my front yard. Nature is moving toward a new season, and it seems the trees are the first to know. They are old and wise. Yes, they know things, these trees.

5

Rain drenched our neighborhood this morning. Our thirsty yards and gardens needed it. Now the sun is out, but the crape myrtle is still drooping, weighed down by rainwater caught in the bunches of blooms that dangle from its branches. The bees don't seem to mind the extra water. Now that the sun is out, each clump of pink blossoms hums with bees busily dipping and gathering. I stand near the mottled brown and rust-red trunk of this leafy, blooming umbrella and look up at its richness, its generous reach, its bountiful bouquets. Then the breeze freshens and tosses the branches. They let loose a shower of rainwater. And I step out into the hot sunshine to drip dry.

6

When I took courses in writing, my mentors, teachers, friends, and I read and discussed many different kinds of books, including some that are commonly called "coming of age" stories. Generally, we think of those as stories of young people, teens going through life experiences that mature them. At their age, they are crossing the bridge from childhood to adulthood. But I think we are always coming of age, moving to the next stage, taking the next step, growing into the future. And the future is something new. Even if we're old, tomorrow is new. Next week is new. Next month? Next year? All new. Whatever age we are, we are always "coming of age."

7

I'm arranging paint sticks and markers, standing them up like little toy soldiers on the tabletop, preparing for my grandson's visit. The last time he was here, he drew on a length of paper cut from a roll that I've had for years. He rolled it out on the floor through the sunroom, across the kitchen, and into the dining room. Then he began drawing a tall man, sunroom-kitchen-dining room tall. So now I'm getting the markers ready for whatever he wants to create today. As I stand these markers side by side with their slick, shiny tops in rows, I realize that I love all colors. Blue is my favorite, for sure, but I love them all. And here they are, in slick, shiny marker tops. The potential they hold inspires me. The anticipation is delicious. Maybe I'm not preparing for my grandson's creative adventures as much as I'm preparing for my own.

8

I have a daydream of the present moment, the now. In that dream, we stand with hands cupped before us, holding what we thought were the thorns of the past. But they've turned into fragrant flowers. As we cradle these flowers in our palms, something marvelous happens: the petals become wings, and with one joyful toss of our cupped hands, we send them flying into the future. And when we lower our hands, we realize that, in spite of everything we let go, our hands are not empty. They are full of mystery and grace and hope enough to fuel our next steps.

9

This morning's sky is overcast
with clouds forming
a vaguely familiar
pattern.
I can't quite place it.

> A jet crosses heading northwest.
> Denver perhaps?
> Another jet follows flying west.
> Maybe Dallas.
> And now I see it,
> that familiar pattern
> in the clouds.
> It's what a giraffe wears
> in brown and yellow.
> We have a white and gray
> giraffe-skin sky.

– kh –

10

Actor and director Michael Chekhov said, "In any true, great piece of art you will always find four qualities which the artist has put into his creation." He calls those qualities the Four Brothers: a feeling of Ease, a feeling of Form, a feeling of Beauty, and a feeling of the Whole. We find Ease, Form, Beauty, and Wholeness not only in great art but in nature as well. These four "brothers" naturally appeal to us. We're attracted to them. I think that's because we, too, are works of art. We are masterpieces.

11

My Goth shamrocks fan out from two pots in two corners of my sun room. Each pot holds about six long stems, each supporting three triangular wine-red leaves that open flat and wide in the daylight and fold inward at night. One pot is perched beside an air vent. When the air blows, cool or warm, the leaves bob and flutter. During the day, when the leaves are open, they look like a flock of wine-red birds. At night, when they fold, they're a flock of butterflies. Gently they fly in place, red birds for daydreams, butterflies for night dreams.

12

I bought a fresh box of crayons, a box of sixty-four, "sharpener included!" When I was growing up, a new box of crayons—especially the big box—made it exciting to buy school supplies. The box lid tilted back, and out wafted a new, waxy smell. It was a box of hope and ambition, a box of anticipation. It was a set of tools that said, "I'm ready for paper of any size, shape or texture. Bring it on." The big box was a collection of names that gave each color a personality: burnt sienna, cornflower, canary. It was a rainbow treasure under a flip-top lid. Opening a new box all these years later, I guess it still is.

13

Go to the pine if you want to learn about the pine.

– Matsuo Basho –

Five pine trees stand in a line across my back fence. I used to think of them as the skinny kids on the block, but they're not kids. They were here before I was. So I'm now calling them the five elders. They are thin and as tall as a four-story house. Two of them lean east; the others grow straight up. I think they're

Eastern White Pines or something related. They produce long, scaly cones, and their reddish-brown, rough, furrowed bark holds a sticky resin with that distinct, clean, crisp pine smell. Their thin, feathery needles grow in fan-like groups that wave to me when a breeze blows through. And when the breeze turns into a stiff wind, these five elders are good at slow-dancing.

14

This morning, the shadows that came in with the sun had a curved upper edge as if the sunlight was shining through an arch. But there was no arch that I could see. The window letting in the light is a large square. No curves there. The neighbor's house, which was reflecting this light into ours, has no curves, at least none that are obvious. But I'm sure there's an explanation. Maybe a trick of the light, the angle of reflections. Or maybe today is simply a day to pay attention to curves.

15

Let us sing a new song
not with our lips but with our lives.

– Saint Augustine –

This morning, I'm grateful for a new day, a new beginning, a fresh start, a sunlit perspective on the worries that seem to darken and deepen at night. This new day is open to possibilities, to fresh grace, to a new song that we sing, as Saint Augustine says, with our lives. Imagine our lives creating music that we could actually hear. What kind of music would it be, I wonder. Maybe each of us would have a different melody, a unique theme. Maybe our activities and times of rest would be variations on that theme. Maybe together we are creating an amazing symphony, one we can't hear but one that echoes through the universe and fills the space between the stars with wonder.

16

The happy highways where I went
And cannot come again.

– A.E. Housman –

Sometimes I find myself in a space of reverie that glances back toward my childhood. It doesn't focus on one or more specific memories but hovers in the ambience of a remembered time. It wraps me in a sense of wonder, expectation, and gratitude and fills me with a light-hearted, hopeful, childlike feeling. I'm not sure what triggers this reverie, this open, expansive, world-at-my-fingertips, fresh-breath feeling. The angle of sunlight? Balmy weather? The dance of a breeze through the trees? What nudges me into this reverie is not something I can specifically point to, and it doesn't really matter, but I keep thinking there must be a word for this kind of ambient memory. Maybe it's what William Faulkner was referring to when he wrote, "Memory believes before knowing remembers." Or maybe it's what Housman calls "happy highways."

17

From my breakfast table, I look out double glass doors that lead to my deck. This morning as I peered out, I noticed that the garden-scape framed by the left window is full of diagonals that lean from the lower left to the upper right of the window, all at different angles: crape myrtle branches, thin and mottled; a faded orange garden stake, tall and wavy; a long, black iron shepherd's crook that holds the hummingbird feeder. These diagonals are all framed by the border around the glass of the door on the left. The right window shows diagonals too, but they lean left: wildflower stems in a large planter; the trunk of a pine tree beyond. Of course, if I change seats at this table or move across the room, this scene will change, the angles will shift, and the asymmetrical symmetry of these diagonals will disappear. But for the moment, I can enjoy this serendipitous gift of nature, this

unique view that only my eyes can see from this one
vantage point on the planet.

18

Four black-eyed Susans,
crones of the planter box,
have lost their golden petals.
Their dark brown seed heads
sit atop tall stalks,
surveying shorter blooms—
pink coneflowers,
sun bright coreopsis,
fluttery white windflowers.
The black-eyes lean toward each other
nodding in the breeze,
garden gossips
sharing the season's secrets.
Shhh! Shhh!
Peace.

– kh –

19

In an abstract art class I once took, the instructor
directed us to create our own abstracts by starting
with a single charcoal line that represented our life

journey. When everyone had finished drawing their lines, we took turns telling, in general, how the lines symbolized our lives. One woman's line wandered all over the paper. Another woman's line spiraled. Another student had drawn smooth curves interrupted with jagged, mountainous sections. It was fascinating to hear my fellow students explain this zig-zag or that curve or the dramatic, bold line that looked as if it fell straight off a cliff. My abstract looked like a roller coaster. Novelist J. Courtney Sullivan said of one of her characters, "She had made a choice and then she had made another and another after that. Taken together, the small choices anyone made added up to a life." My choices had added up to a life.

20

Hope is
the expectant yes of our spirits,
the energy that propels us forward,
the anticipation of good to come,
our "all shall be well,"
the pull of possibility, of life expanding,
the window of the soul looking toward renaissance,
curiosity and wonder,
confidence in grace unfolding,
the invitation of tomorrow's gifts,
the deep breath and fresh air of a new day.

– kh –

21

I don't know the sea well, but I've visited its shores more than once. I'm fascinated by its sandy beaches, its rocky banks, its tide pools and inlets. When I close my eyes, I can hear its rushing, shushing voice. I've collected some of the sea's wonders in a box. They were once cradled within the sea's flow, deep in its darkness with sunlight filtering down—a sea star, a sand dollar, a conch that holds the echo of waves. I enjoy the sea mostly from its edge, looking out to the place where it appears to give way to sky. But I know it doesn't give way. It surges on and on, arms wide, singing its wild, crashing song. I once saw a storm approaching from the far horizon of the sea, roiling its dark surface. The sea frightens me and delights me and challenges me and comforts me. I am in awe of the sea.

22

I have no time to grow old. . . .
I am too busy for that.

– George MacDonald –

In a sense, time is a god. We're ruled by it, bow to it, and rely on it as we consult our calendars. Time is a currency—we "spend" it. In fact, we're rich with it. Everyone is. No one else owns more minutes than anyone else. Each of us literally has all the time that exists right now in the whole world. The thing is, we can't stop it or call "time out." Time doesn't ask any of us whether we want to go for a ride; it just picks us up and carries us along. And it's up to us to make the best of it.

23

Oh, dear cat,
you've come in with a white feather
over your gray eyebrow.
Did it tumble onto you from above?
Was it stuck in a shrub?
Did it catch on your fur
when you passed underneath?
Oh, dear feather,
where did you come from?
Was there a battle?
A falcon?
A hawk?
Did you fall from the winner?
Do you signal a loss?
Or—I hesitate to ask—
is this cat
who purrs so gently in my lap
a prrreditor?
– kh –

24

A few years ago, when I was studying watercolor, I commented that my paintings never turned out like what I had envisioned. The teacher, a gracious, generous, and accomplished artist, said, "If you know what your painting is going to look like, why paint?" Not knowing is part of the adventure and magic of art. It's a bit like life. We're all headed toward some destination that we can't yet see. What's past lies behind us. What's present envelopes us. What will be . . . no one knows. But not knowing is part of the adventure.

25

The early morning sunlight often tries to trick me by shining into my house from the west, not the east. It's an illusion created by reflections. Before the sun is high enough to shine through my east windows, it hits my neighbor's house, which sits to the west of mine. That light reflects off the neighbor's windows and siding to beam into my house. Sneaky. It's as if the sun is rising in the west. Hello, sun. I'm onto your tricks.

26

The sky is mauve tonight with lavender clouds that gradually gray as the sun sinks below the horizon. For some reason, I think of satin. Maybe the sky reminds me of a satin pillowcase I once slept on. It was lavender-gray and as soft as rose petals. And that is tonight's sky—mauve satin, soft as petals, soft as a pillow.

27

You will find something more in woods than in books.
Trees and stones will teach you
that which you can never learn from masters.

– St. Bernard of Clairvaux –

Trees hold stories. The huge tulip poplar in my front yard was just a twig when my oldest son brought it home from school on Arbor Day. We stuck it in the ground not expecting it to grow. The dogwood nearby was planted by former owners of our house in memory of a grandmother. The hackberry in our backyard held a treehouse for so many years that the floor of the treehouse buckled as the tree trunk expanded. Even the footstool that my granny made out of a tree stump could tell a few stories if it could talk. I have no idea where the stump came from, but

I wish I knew. I wish I had thought to ask her. Trees hold stories. Some of them are secret.

28

We all have our time machines.
Those that take us back are memories.
And those that carry us forward are dreams.

– The Time Machine movie –
based on the novel by H.G. Wells

Between memories and dreams, there's a path we're walking, the present moment. Memories are behind us; dreams are ahead somewhere. Our present journey touches both, but it's in the Now that we can make a difference. It's now that we choose which direction to point our feet. Each of us navigates life as best we can. What matters is how we travel, what we discover along the way, what we choose to carry with us, and what we choose to leave behind.

29

We don't rest from our work;
we work from our rest.

– Jayson D. Bradley –

As I vacuumed my floors yesterday, I realized that my vacuum cleaner works on the rest/work principle. It's cordless and has to charge up before it can work. When it runs low, it has to be recharged before it can work again. It works from rest. No rest, no work. I like this different way of viewing my nightly eight hours. It's the beginning instead of the end. It's a prioritized gift of time, relaxing at the start instead of rewarding myself with rest at the end of the day. Of course, there's no right or wrong way to look at it. Work, then rest? Or rest, then work? Either view makes sense. But working from rest puts a bit more emphasis on the resting. I'm charging up.

30

Sonoran Desert, Arizona, September 2012

A hot, dry breeze ruffles my hair as I shade my eyes and scan the sapphire-blue sky and the surrounding hills covered with scrub brush, ocotillo, and stick figure saguaro. My three younger sisters have splurged for my sixtieth birthday and are treating me to a week with them at a resort and spa, an oasis of porches, pools, palm trees, and paths. I love the dry heat. I love the wide sky. I love my sisters.

When we arrived at the resort, we got to choose from the usual spa offerings plus hikes, trail rides, and an intriguing session called the equine experience. "Work with specially selected horses and our expert facilitators," the description read, "getting a chance to notice personal patterns of learned behavior that may be holding you back from the life you want to live." It had been awhile since I'd been with horses, and this seemed like a good time of life to learn what might be holding me back, so I signed up.

Which is why I'm now standing in the corral, eyeing the desert hills as I bake in the sun. I turn back to the horse I've chosen to work with. She's the oldest horse here, so I feel some connection, seeing as how I'm moving into senior territory myself. At the moment, my job is to clean her front left hoof. The underneath part. So I have to get her to raise her leg. But she's not cooperating. Her feet stay firmly planted on the ground.

"I don't think she wants to do this," I tell the trainer. "At least she doesn't want me to do this."

"It's not about the horse," says the trainer. "She knows the drill. Just touch her on her foreleg, and she'll raise her foot for you."

I touch. Nothing happens. I think it's obvious that she doesn't want to raise her foot right now. But I say nothing and try again. No go. Maybe I'm doing this wrong. I stroke her and try again. Nothing. I resist peeking at the other participants with their horses, but I'm afraid that I'll be the only person here who can't get their horse's hooves clean.

"Okay, step back," says the trainer. "Deep breath. What are you thinking?"

I inhale deeply, exhale slowly. "Umm, I'm thinking I can't make her raise her foot if she doesn't want to." Plus, I'm no good at this, I think; plus, I'm afraid I'll fail; plus . . .

"She'll do it," says the trainer. "She likes having her hoof cleaned. But she can sense what you're feeling. Give yourself a minute and try again."

I look to the hills, breathe deeply, let all those thoughts fly off into the desert somewhere, and start over. I try not to think at all but simply approach the horse as if I do this every day. I touch her foreleg, and—wonder of wonders!—she lifts her foot and lets me scrape her hoof clean.

"What was different that time?" asks the trainer.

At that moment, I know the secret: I gave up control. I, who have made a career out of thinking, stopped thinking for a moment. I let go of the outcome, touched the horse, and, with her cooperation, bent to my work. As I relaxed into the moment, into my surroundings, into the experience, so did the horse.

Autumn

OCTOBER

1

Nature's peace will flow into you
as sunshine flows into trees.
The winds will blow their own freshness into you,
and the storms their energy,
while cares will drop away from you
like the leaves of Autumn.

– John Muir –

Exhale worry and inhale nature's faithful beauty. Exhale confusion and inhale nature's clarity. Exhale tension and inhale nature's comfort. Exhale staleness and let the wind blow its freshness into you. Let your cares drop away like the leaves of autumn.

2

In Lisa Dale's book about writing memoir, she encourages writers to look back at the events of their life and "line them up in some pattern that offers grace for all involved." We can do the same even if we're not writing a memoir. We can choose how to line up the memories. We can choose a view that offers grace. Isn't that what we're to be about—grace for all involved?

3

I saw old Autumn in the misty morn
stand shadowless like silence, listening
to silence.

– Thomas Hood –

I woke up this morning to a world washed in fog. Backyard elms, wearing a veil of mist, stretch toward the clouded sky as if they're looking for a missing sun that they know is up there somewhere. The roofs of backyard neighbors seem sleepy, still abed under a filmy blanket, and over the roofs, trees rise in muted, dusty gray. Beyond, on the next block, a line of treetops that's usually bright with sunrise is barely visible as a faint outline in this soft cotton, smoky wonder of nature, this light warm cloak that dawn is wearing. It's a slow, quiet start to the day. It's a morning hug of fog.

4

There will come a time
when you believe everything is finished.
That will be the beginning.

– Louis L'Amour –

What looks like the end is simply the beginning. I think that's the lesson of autumn as the leaves drop away and the trees go bare, as flowers wilt and dry and fall from their stems, as birds fly south and the winds grow cold. Even the calendar year heads into its last pages. It would be easy to believe that everything is finished. But we've been around long enough, haven't we, to know that it's just the beginning.

5

A man sees in the world what he carries in his heart.

– Johann Wolfgang von Goethe –

A friend recently confided in me that she was disillusioned. She sounded sad, disappointed, discouraged. And I felt sad with her. But the more I thought about it, the more I realized that dis-illusionment is not a bad thing. It's simply getting rid of illusions. Stripping away pretense. Ditching fallacies. Dismantling deception. Dis-illusioned, we can see what is truly of value. For me at this moment, that's the ground I'm standing on, the air I'm breathing, the chirp of chickadees at the bird feeder, the scent of jasmine tea in my cup, the rustle of leaves in the wind, and the thought of you on the other side of this strand of words. Some people may prefer illusion, but illusion is never a solid support. The truth is, what we hold in our hearts will, in the end, hold us. An illusion won't be strong enough to hold us well. It's a mirage. But reality will hold. The wonders of nature, the treasures of joy, peace, kindness, and love—these are real. These are solid. These will hold.

6

Today I saw a maple tree that looked like it couldn't make up its mind. The leaves on the upper half of the tree were red, while its lower leaves were green. It's as if part of the tree wanted to welcome autumn and the other part wanted to stay with summer a bit longer. Neither of them has won that disagreement yet. Maybe they decided to settle it by simply being two colors. Why not? I must say, it's beautiful.

7

Rain is falling straight down in thin silver streaks, making a hushed patter on the roof and deck boards. As I watch, it becomes heavier and heavier until it blurs the trees. Then it calms again into a quiet patter. A light, cool breeze flows through open windows. Droplets hang like a fringe of diamonds along the deck rail and bird feeder. The bamboo bows. The crape myrtle seeds are weighed down and drip in little splashes on the soaked deck. A bird calls, "Clear, clear, clear." The rainstorm is over.

8

Squirrel highways run through our trees, on top of the garage roof, across electrical wires, and along our fence. I suspect the squirrels can get all the way around the neighborhood without ever touching the ground. They run in short scrambles and hops, always alert for cats and dogs and hawks, and I guess if they stay out long enough in the evening, they have to watch for coyotes and owls as well. Squirrels can be pests. But they have their good qualities too. Last year a squirrel planted me an entire patch of sunflowers.

9

This morning, I noticed how magical the light of dawn looks peeking through the stand of bamboo beside my house. It twinkled like party lights as a breeze swayed the tall stalks and riffled through the slim leaves. Then I noticed the diagonal stripes of shadow that the sun and bamboo were creating across the driveway. The bamboo and the rising sun—they play together beautifully.

10

Clouds are sailing slowly northeast like little flotillas in the upper reaches of the sky. Their slowness surprises me, because down here on the ground, the wind is strong and gusty. I suspect the clouds are moving faster than I think. They do progress steadily and seem to be determined to block out the sun. As it turns out, this flotilla is the vanguard, the leading edge of an entire swath of clouds. Farewell for today, sun. Maybe we'll see you again tomorrow when these ships have sailed.

11

The afternoon sun is easing in through the west windows in my bedroom, shining a narrow rhombus of light on my bed. The wind is grand today, gusting and whirling outdoors, tossing tree branches that wave in shadows across the patch of light, making it flicker. Rushing, surging, ebbing, the wind sounds like the sea. If I didn't know I was in Nashville, I'd think I was in a beach house listening to the ocean. Shh, it says. Shh. Listen. Rest. I might take its advice. I might rest in a rhombus of light.

12

In the twilight of dawn, I lie in bed and let the cool breeze brush over me as I listen to the world outside my open windows. The first thing I hear is a soft underlying swish like a gentle tide, maybe wind in the trees, maybe cars on the distant freeway. Around six o'clock, a jet crosses the sky with a hum that rises in a momentary crescendo and then fades away. A car rushes down the street. A bird twitters somewhere in the distance. Another one answers closer in. The cat jumps off the bed with a light thud. There's a distant pulsing beep of a truck backing up and a growing river of traffic on the freeway a couple of miles north. An insect begins a high-pitched hum. Another jet flies overhead with a whine. Another bird joins in the morning song, another car swishes as it passes by. Chirps and faint rumbles drift in. I add a rustle of sheets, a stretch, and a deep breath. My bed creaks as I rise. The world is waking up.

13

My youngest grandson found several baby-pea size crape myrtle seeds fallen on the back deck. He gathered four of them and immediately wanted to plant them. I said he could but cautioned him that they might not grow. He strategically chose his spots:

two in the center of the back yard, one in a brush pile in the side yard, and one by the back patio. Then he found one more seed and asked me to plant it—again, in the middle of the yard. I took my time, changed the subject, hoped he would forget. He didn't. So I let him show me the spot. I dug through the grass into the dark brown clayish soil and planted it. Why not? You never know. Trees do grow from seeds.

14

This afternoon, the wind is rushing in one window and out the other. As it passes by, it tosses loose papers from my desk to the floor. It rattles papers held down by paperweights and a paper clip jar. It ruffles a peacock feather stuck in a cup of pens, pencils, and scissors. It whistles and moans. It's a wild wind. But it also feels cleansing, fresh and cool. And it makes me wonder—what's blowing in?

15

In the wee hours of the morning, shortly after
midnight, a cold front blew in. I had all my windows
open to the mild, humid evening. But with gusts that
ebbed and flowed like sea waves crashing into rocks,
the temperature changed. Cold air billowed in, and I
pulled up my covers. The cat nosed her way under
too, and there we lay listening to the whine and howl,
the surge and splash of wind.

16

Oh, better than the minting
of a gold-crowned king
Is the safe-kept memory
Of a lovely thing.

– Unknown –

Ethel's small front yard, enclosed by a white picket
fence, was completely planted in roses. Their perfume
enveloped me all the way up her front sidewalk and
followed me into her house in Hollywood, California,
where neighborhoods of quaint, old houses lie tucked
between busy streets. This was many years ago when
I lived in LA and visited elderly people who were no
longer able to attend the church I went to. Ethel was

about ninety years old, could not see well, and did not get out often. So I went to her.

Every table and shelf at Ethel's house was full of small knickknacks. She often pointed me to the mantle and asked if her collection of cloisonné was still there. She recounted stories of her travels, mentioned her "beau" of long ago, and told me about the time in her childhood when a mattress, set out to air on her front porch, began to bulge and ripple all by itself. Some said the mattress was "hainted" by a ghost—until they discovered a snake inside it. The thought had me shivering as much as if it truly had been "hainted."

Ethel, her roses, and her stories are for me a safe-kept memory of a lovely thing.

17

I've been thinking a lot about seeds this week. Red berries are plumping out on my honeysuckle and nandina. My magnolia has loosed her seeds. The coneflowers are fading, leaving their prickly seed heads behind, and the poppies seeded some time ago, the tiny holes atop their globe-shaped pods providing an escape route for their even tinier black seeds. My garden is maturing. I'm saying, "Same time next year" to the perennials. But I'm saying goodbye to the annuals. Unless they seed themselves, they won't return next year. It will soon be time for most of my garden to rest.

18

A squirrel is rasping and chirring, fussing at my cat. A chipmunk is sounding his warning too, a continual, squeaky chip-chip-chip. I can see the squirrel hunkered down in a tree branch, but I can't see the chipmunk. He's somewhere nearby but well hidden. I've previously seen him peeking out of our next-door neighbor's drainpipe. Maybe he's there but farther in this time, trying to warm up on this chilly, clear-sky day. Or almost clear-sky. One lone white puff of a cloud is making its way eastward. Is it a scout for clouds that will follow, or is it a straggler left behind? Maybe it's just a loner, feeling its freedom and enjoying the space. Like my cat.

19

As I wrap a set of fancy placemats, a gift for a friend, I notice a variety of textures. The slick, thin plastic wrap that protects the placemats is cool and slides beneath my fingers. I wrap it in thin tissue paper, smoothing and creasing it. The crinkly sound attracts my cat, who snoops around the edges, sniffing at it, no doubt thinking, what's this? Are we playing? When it looks like play is not on the agenda, she pads away in search of other adventures. I now wrap the package in a top layer of bright pink paper that feels slightly rough as I run my hand over it. The tape is sticky as I tear it off the dispenser but smooth as I press it on the package and rub it down. I press two pink, satiny bows on top. In the overhead light, they shine almost as if they have a light of their own. And here's my friend's gift, a textured wonder, wrapped at every point with good wishes and love.

20

It's morning, but the sun has not yet risen above the bamboo. It's still that "magical hour" of dimness as the days grow darker and the sun rises later. As I set the table for breakfast, I notice that on the back deck, the mandevilla vine seems to be loving this cool weather. It's full of white trumpet-like blooms with yellow throats. As I'm admiring them, a bright yellow catches my eye. It's on the next street over, between the houses of my backyard neighbors. It's the only thing bright at this dusky time of morning: a brilliant yellow tree. It glows as if the neighbors have turned a spotlight on it. Then I realize that, yes, a spotlight is on it. It's nature's spotlight. The rising sun has found a gap in the line of trees and roofs and has beamed its brilliance onto this one tree.

21

I was driving home after spending the day at my younger son's house when I discovered that I had left my cell phone there. I was miffed and on the verge of crying—it had been a long day, I was tired, it was rush hour, I was hungry and looking forward to just chilling after dinner, but I still had to make dinner. Now I'd have to turn around. But then I took a deep breath and decided to go home and drive the thirty minutes back to my son's house after dinner, after rush hour. And that's what I did. After dinner, I headed back across town. It was just after sunset. I began to watch the roads darken and notice the headlights and tail lights, the double yellow stripe on my left, the white stripe at the edge of the road on my right, the silhouettes of trees against the darkening sky, and stretches of road where I was the only car for a minute or two. I remembered E.L. Doctorow's famous statement: "Writing is like driving at night. You can see only as far as your headlights, but you can make the whole trip that way." And the evening softened. So did my tension. I breathed easily. I'd been here before, lived most of my life this way, the old way, without a phone, without connection, just the peace of me and the road.

22

The weather is quite balmy for late October. The nights are chilly, but the days are still warm. On the way to the mailbox, I stopped to take a picture of a fresh-faced violet among the brittle, brown fallen leaves. Then I saw another violet. And another. I counted five. The rhododendron had buds too, one with a pink petal peeking out. I expect it will bloom before the end of the week. It's a bit of spring in autumn, and I'm happy to see it.

23

October's full moon is the Hunter's Moon. Last year I saw it as it rose, huge and round and orange. I'm going to try to catch it again this year with my camera. I'm going to hunt the Hunter before the North Wind takes a bite out of it.

24

It's a windy morning but as mild as spring, and I'm walking to church. White clouds with light gray underbellies meander across the sky on currents of air. I pass a "tarzan vine" hanging from a tall hedge of wild honeysuckle and white, dainty frostweed. Light purple American asters are bunched along the sidewalk. Once in a while among the drifts of brown, crisp leaves on the ground, there's one that's brilliant red or vibrant yellow. A lone mockingbird is going through his repertoire of songs on my side of the street as two chattery birds flutter out and back on the other side. Runners are out, jogging down the sidewalk. I greet my neighbor walking his dog. I pause at a Southern magnolia to get a good look at one of its fuzzy seed cones with bright red seeds emerging. And in the church garden, fall-blooming azaleas are in their bright pink Sunday best. I've not even stepped into the building, and already I feel generously blessed.

25

A few years ago, a friend and I were treated to a peaceful week of writing at a resort in Hilton Head. The balconies of our third-floor rooms looked down onto a walkway bordered in trees and flowers. On the first night of our stay, my friend called me to her balcony window and silently pointed to a tree. Through the dark, I could barely see a white form the size of a small hawk, resting in the branches. "Is it a bird?" she asked. "A possum? A raccoon?" I squinted at the creature, which shifted slightly, but I couldn't make out a definite shape. My friend concluded that whatever it was, it was sitting on a nest. After watching a while longer, we gave up on getting a clearer view. The next morning, my friend called me to her window again. "It's still there!" she said. I looked, and there it was. A plastic grocery bag caught in the branches, shifting slightly in the breeze.

26

On a withered branch
A crow has settled—
Autumn nightfall.

– Matsuo Basho, translated by Einbond –

I've often wished that I had a skylight in the ceiling over my bed so that I could look up at the stars at night or maybe see clouds through it in the morning. It's an extravagant wish and not very affordable. But last night when I got in bed and turned off the light, there it was, spanning the entire ceiling—not a real skylight but one made of light and shadow. My neighbors to the west had left a light on outdoors, and it was glowing through my windows, creating an elongated window shape overhead. Shadow and light had filled my whole ceiling with a skylight. Extravagant. And free.

27

I found a Y under my refrigerator. I had noticed the edge of it peeking out and bent down to retrieve it. My grandchildren had been playing with magnetic words and letters, and this one obviously got lost. Now I'm wondering what else might be hiding under the refrigerator. Maybe I should do a bit of cleaning. I might find out "Y" something I lost long ago went missing.

28

A steady silver rain is streaking like tears down the windowpane. The cat mews to go out even though she can surely see and hear the raindrops. When I open the door, she stares in disbelief. It's true. Rain. The air is chilled though not yet frosty. She shivers and turns back to the warm, dry safety of indoors. Outdoors, the fall blooms seem glad. The yellow and pink mums lift their faces to the skies and drink.

29

Mint is still growing in a wide pot on my deck. As I was clearing withered stems from the pot beside the mint, I happened to brush against it and was immediately treated to its bright, clean fragrance. It was an invitation to pause, and I did. I pinched off a wrinkled mint leaf to smell it again. What a marvel. Before there was mint chocolate chip ice cream or thin mints or mint tea or minty toothpaste, mint was simply a plant growing here and there, generously gifting the world with its sparkling smell.

30

I found a poplar seed pod under the tulip poplar today. It's flame-shaped, brown and woody, and layered with zig-zag sections, a bit like a pine cone but smoother and smaller. The tulip poplar has been in my front yard for thirty-five years, blooming in yellow, tulip-shaped blossoms with orange heart-shaped markings on their inner petals. Why have I never noticed these amazing seed pods before? It makes me wonder what else is underfoot, at hand, right before my eyes, calling to my ear . . . and I've never noticed?

31

There's a warm sun today but a strong, chilly breeze. The leaves that are still in the trees are crisp-edged, enjoying their last days on their branches. Many have already fallen. Many more will likely fall today, blown to the ground by this wind that has me pulling my sweater close around me on my walk. The squatty redbud trees are thinning. Their remaining heart-shaped leaves are gold-green and freckled with brown. Dark brown seed pods hang in fringes along their branches. Once in a while a yellow leaf twirls down to join the other leaves already piled up on the sidewalk. The overnight wind and rain has blown down twiggy branches onto the sidewalk. Droplets puddle on golden leaves scattered along the way. There could be no more perfect gifts for me today. And I am grateful.

NOVEMBER

1

November is a wise old woman
weaving words of wisdom
from a skein of experience
in the colors of sadness
and joy.

– kh –

2

This week, a friend told me that she loves winter-bare trees, because they reveal their true shape, their curves and angles. I love budding springtime trees. I also love billowy, leafy summer trees. I love red and gold autumn trees. But I do enjoy the patterns that winter-bare trees make silhouetted against the sky. Their branches are like lace and lattice. Their bark reddens in the splash of sunrise and the glow of sunset. They sparkle with frost. Now that I think of it, I love winter-bare trees too.

3

Tonight I was doing a final cleaning of my studio when car headlights out the side window caught my eye. I paused to watch a car pull up to my neighbor's curb. No one got out. They had probably stopped to check their phone messages or confirm an address. Meanwhile, their headlights were shining on two sprinklers in the neighbor's yard. The light glinted off the fountain-like spray, making the water sparkle as it whirled around, flinging out silver cascades. The moment was magical. Then the car moved on, the silver cascades disappeared into darkness, and I went back to cleaning paintbrushes.

4

In Frederick Buechner's novel *Godric*, he wrote a wise and gracious truth: "[A]ll the death that ever was, set next to life, would scarce fill a cup." Once in a while, I have to remind myself of that truth. All the ugliness that ever was, all the unkindness, all the destruction, all the death fade to insignificance next to beauty and kindness, love, and life.

5

The seasons alter: hoary-headed frosts
Fall in the fresh lap of the crimson rose.

– Shakespeare –

A torn-out page from a magazine was tacked to the wall above the table of my grandmother's kitchen at the ranch (my grandad was a cowboy). It was a picture of an artist's imagination of Jack Frost. I don't know why Grandmother chose to tack that particular picture to the wall, but it appealed to my preschool self. Scroll ahead to this morning when that memory came tumbling back. I woke up warm under my covers, but getting up was a shivery affair. I raised my window shades and looked out the upstairs windows. Frost had tipped the neighbor's grass white. The same icy white had dusted their dark brown shingles, making it look as if someone had sprinkled sugar over layers of chocolate. Of course, I knew who had done all this. Jack Frost had visited our neighborhood during the night.

6

The higher your structure is to be,
the deeper must be its foundation.

– St. Augustine –

At Cheekwood Botanical Gardens, I occasionally walk the Sculpture Trail. As its name suggests, the trail winds past various sculptures on its way through the woods that curve around the outer edge of the gardens. At one point, large tree roots jut up and out in a jumble across the dirt path. These great knees and elbows of roots rise and dip and curve and cross. I watch my footing and pick my way through. The woods feel ancient. It's a great privilege to see these old roots. I know that they have other roots going deep, deep, deep down. So it feels like these are a bit of a gift, a secret revealed. Grow tall, they say. Dance with the breeze. Bend with the wind. And stay rooted.

7

Morning dawns clear, cloudless, and cold. I see it through the double windows in front of my desk. Twelve panes divide the outdoor autumn scene into twelve panels. Each pane is a picture on its own. The bottom six show rooftops and neighboring trees. The middle six show elm trunks and a maze of branches splashed with leaves. The top six show treetops and sky. All together, they reveal a peaceful scene of this new day.

8

As I rinsed the dishes this morning, I admired the way the overhead light gleamed on the shoulders of a soft-soap bottle. Then I began noticing other shoulder curves and the way they reflected light. Or not. The shrug of a salt shaker. The slim shoulders of a bud vase with a handle that gives it the look of having one hand on its hip. The drop-shouldered tea kettle. The stiff, knobby shoulders of a chair at the breakfast table. The padded shoulders of an armchair. I thought about my own shoulders—slumped, pulled back, tensed, shrugging, shimmying, angled one up, one down. And I realized something: The shoulders of a bottle reflect light. Our shoulders reflect our feelings.

9

The clock ticks quietly
mid-morning
on this day that's sunny
with a thin layer of clouds.
It's warm enough for open windows.
A light breeze drifts in.
Outside it's flicking leaves off the trees.
They tumble,
somersault,
land with soft clicks,

rattle to a stop and settle,
only to be scooped up
by a sudden gust
that skitters them,
scatters them,
tumbles them
into a pile against the fence.
The elm is speckled with the hangers-on,
the last to let go.
Soon it will be empty
of leaves.
The clock ticks
quietly toward noon.

– kh –

10

I looked up from my desk this afternoon to see four vapor trails, fat and fuzzy, fanning out like rays from a child-drawn sun hidden somewhere behind the crown of the neighbor's oak tree. It's kind of a "choose your own adventure" collection of trails. Follow the path into the sun (where one of these trails appears to lead). Or trace the path to the oak tree. Or streak along this trail into the wild blue yonder (where the longest of the vapor trails is headed). I'm thinking poetically, of course, but it occurs to me that the literal view is not so different. Those vapor trails don't lead to the sun or the oak tree, but they do sail the wild blue yonder. And just think of all the people who took those paths, all the people who have chosen their own adventure today.

11

The neighbors who live cattycorner across the street from us are getting a small porch awning built over their front steps. It reminds me of the bill of a ball cap. The neighbors to our east have a covered porch the size of a small room with a swing at one end. The neighbors to the west have what I think of as a storybook porch. It's small and entered through a bricked arch. When I knock on their front door, it feels secret and secluded. Our front porch has no ball-cap awning. It has no archway. It's not room-size. It's not even covered. It's just up three steps to a small concrete landing—exactly like our cattycorner neighbors' porch before they got their ball cap. Maybe we should follow suit?

12

It's a wild-wind morning. Rippled layers of clouds scoot across the sky, their front edges silver, their bellies gray. The pine trees' branches bob like wings as if they're trying to lift the whole tree up and fly away. But the tree top is swaying side to side as if to say, "No, we're staying rooted today." And I hope they do.

13

This morning as the sun was edging over the stand of bamboo, tipping the trees with golden light, I filled the birdbath, which was, unusually, completely empty and dry. As the water poured in, it began to steam into a rising mist that dissipated as it rose. What a beautiful way to begin the day.

14

These are the gold and russet days when I wake up to a window view of leaves lit fiery by the morning sun. The trees are turning color late, losing leaves now instead of in October. While the elms and hackberries are almost bare, the oak is just now turning a golden color tipped with orange. Maple reds are now easing into russet. Late, I was thinking. All late. Then I read a social-media post by Bernice Rocque, who describes herself as a writer, gardener, and family historian: "Such glorious and long color change this year," she wrote. Ah, perspective. I'm changing my assessment. The color change is not late. It's simply long and glorious.

15

My son who lived in Japan for several years told me that if you look carefully at Japanese art, you'll often see a path or bridge that curves over the horizon or around a bend. The bridge is a symbol of the unknown that lies ahead. As I look toward my own future, toward the curve in the path, toward the disappearing bridge, the far edges of my feelings curl like the tattered border of an ancient map. I wonder if this is how early explorers felt when they headed into uncharted territory: excitement and panic, energy and overwhelm, anticipation and dread. Here there be dragons—or not. All I know to do is look carefully and approach the bridge one step at a time.

16

This morning, the sunrise spread its usual sunny-day shadow of our trees across the neighbor's house. I wondered, what if the house were not there? The shadow would fall to the ground to make dusky rivulets in the grass. But what if the ground were not there? What if the tree sat on the edge of a cliff at the Grand Canyon? The shadow would land far away on whatever outcropping might catch it. And yet between the outcropping and the tree, the shadow would drift unseen in the air. If a plane were to cross its path, the shadow would show up, however momentarily, on the plane. So the air is full of shadows, but they need something to catch them, surfaces to stretch across—like us. Sometimes we're the surface, and we catch shadows. Or maybe they catch us.

17

Rain is slowly dripping down the window panes this morning. The sky is a soft silvery gray, lighter overhead, with darker, lower, wooly-edged clouds gliding in from the west. A flock of birds in silhouette darts low between trees, flying from one shelter to another. Wind is gently tossing the branches of the pines, which are still green, although they've shed a thick carpet of gold needles. The way they're nodding, they look as if they're pronouncing a solemn benediction over the gold needles, their precious gift to autumn.

18

Go forth under the open sky,
and listen to Nature's teachings.

– William Cullen Bryant –

What is Nature teaching me? To listen, I think. The world will circle on with or without me. The evening star will rise. Clouds will sail the skies. Cicadas will buzz. Crickets will chirp. Trees will dance in the wind. Seasons will glide in and then pass on. Nature says to simply breathe deeply and listen.

19

It's 3:30 a.m., and I'm late getting up. I peer out to see if there's anything left of the near total eclipse of the moon. Apparently, the eclipse is almost over, and I've missed the main act. At this point, the moon looks like a white Mandarin orange slice in the sky. But I watch long enough to see the earth's shadow move and the white slice of moon grow larger and wider as we here on earth move out of the way of the sun's rays. Then I head back to bed. It's 3:50 a.m. I'm not done with sleep. And sleep is not done with me.

20

It's a sunny, fresh, breezy day. The yards are full of leaves. The elms are bare now, and the poplar is more branch than leaf. But the rhododendron is still showy with three clusters of magenta blooms. A yellow begonia blossom, probably the last of the season, is peeking out at autumn as crape myrtle leaves, gold and red, rain down in the soft drift of wind. Today is all whoosh and bird chirps and breeze. It's a whispery day.

21

I'm knitting a sweater, an overlarge, bulky thing in a soft gray, thick yarn. The whole effort is a sensory experience from the click and glide of the aluminum needles to the soft, texture of the yarn that goes taut and then slack with each stitch. As one row knits into the next, the pattern begins to reveal itself in interlocking rows, ribbed and smooth. When I'm done, I plan to wear it on chilly days like this one. I expect it will be a warm, snugly hug.

22

Appreciate. I'm hearing that word often among my friends these days. We're all working together on some challenging projects, and I count myself lucky to have their talented, smart help. I also count myself lucky that they are all grateful people who are quick to tell each other, *Thanks. I appreciate your help*. The meaning of appreciate hides at its center: prec, from the Latin word for price. Price, prize, praise, precious—they're all related. So when I say I appreciate you reading this, it's my way of saying I value you. I prize you. I praise you. You are precious. I appreciate you.

23

Sharon Salzberg, who teaches mindfulness meditation, suggests that we make a habit of breathing deeply with this thought: "May I be safe, may I be well, may I be happy, may I be at ease." I go a bit further and give it a couple of tweaks.

May I be peaceful. May you be peaceful. May all beings be peaceful.
May I be joyful. May you be joyful. May all things be joyful.

May I be healthy. May you be healthy. May all things be healthy.

May I be safe. May you be safe. May all things be safe.

May I be at peace. May you be a peace. May all things be at peace.

24

The sunlight on my neighbor's yellow-gold tree looks incandescent, glowing like a candle flame. Its upper limbs are still full of foliage, bunched and bountiful, although the lower limbs have lost so many leaves that those remaining are spaced like scattered golden mosaic tiles. With each breath of wind, a few flutter down. But this tree is holding on as if it's been chosen by all the trees to represent them as the bright one this season.

25

A tiny oak tree has planted itself in my front garden near the porch steps. That happens once in a while. A maple sprouted in the middle of my iris bed. A mimosa came up under a hackberry. Last year, an oak grew into a sapling at the side of my back yard. I was hopeful that I could let it grow undisturbed. But my neighbor needed to build a fence to keep his dog in, and the oak would have been in the way. I know that more oaks and maples and mimosas will sprout here and there, and I might as well get used to pulling them up. I think my impulse to save them comes from a scarcity of trees where I grew up in West Texas. So I want all of these to grow. I want the impossible. Sorry, I tell the little oak by the front porch. And I go to get the shovel.

26

Raindrops are dancing on the windows, spangling the screens, dripping from the eaves. It's a soggy day. Cardinals and blue jays are still flitting from branch to branch, darting from tree to tree, plucking seeds from the feeders. But I wonder about birds in the rain. The drops roll off their oily feathers, I think. Still, one raindrop to them must feel like what we'd experience getting splashed with a whole cup of water. A whole rainstorm must be daunting. But they obviously find places to take shelter, because when the clouds scatter, they're back at the feeders. They know how to carry on.

27

All the leaves of the pepper plants and mandevilla vine and butterfly milkweed are drooping, their shoulders slumped as if to say they've finally given up and given in to the reality of approaching winter. "Okay," they seem to say. "We've delayed bedtime as long as we can, and now it's time for our long winter's nap." Some in my garden will return next spring. Some will reseed themselves and multiply and pop back up in surprising places. Others will simply be gone, and it will be up to me to replant.

28

As I drove to my son's house, I saw something that I hadn't seen in a long while: a murmuration of birds. There were hundreds, a dark cloud of them, flocked together, flying in one direction. The cloud thinned and thickened as they flew, gliding slightly apart, then closing ranks. Over and over, they parted and closed in, parted and closed in. Then in a flash, all as one, they changed directions. This dark cloud that had been sailing south was now flying north. Until, in another flash, they once again headed south.

29

My youngest grandson was spending the day at my house recently, and he was having a fairly normal day that involved the usual variety of feelings: adventure, boredom, cooperation, and stubbornness. At one point, he straddled the rail of the banister and said, "Mimi, you're on my don't-like-do-like list." I patted his back. "That's the way it is lots of times with family," I said. "They're don't-like-do-like people. I'm happy to be one of yours."

30

It is the sky that makes the earth so lovely at sunrise, and so splendid at sunset.
In the one it breathes over the earth the crystal-like ether,
in the other liquid gold.

– painter Thomas Cole –

A wondrous sky greets this cold, crisp morning. It's criss-crossed with contrails, probably due to holiday travel. Toward the horizon, a wide sweep of thin, feathery clouds spans the blue like a skyscape dry-brushed in white across a deep blue canvas. All this, and the sun is still on the rise. It's painting tree tops gold, while their lower trunks and branches rest in twilight shadow. The sky is breathing over the earth, waking it up with beauty.

DECEMBER

The aspens at the cross-roads talk together
Of rain, until their last leaves fall from the top.

– Edward Thomas –

The leaves on my cannas have turned yellow and red and look like big flames. They rarely bloom. They're under a hackberry, so I suspect they don't get enough sun to flower. But their leaves thrive, returning year after year. My dad always said it was hard to kill a canna. In spring, they emerge from the ground rolled up like a diploma and slowly unfurl to become deep green, floppy summertime leaves. This time of year, the leaves turn yellow and red, and sunrise and sunset make them glow like stained glass windows. Until winter blows in, icy cold. Then they'll dry to a warm brown, wither, and droop on their stalks like a flag on a still day. But that's just a different kind of beauty. I'll leave them where they are until they need to be cleared out for spring.

2

My husband called me to the back porch this evening to see an opossum on the steps leading down to the driveway. By the time I stepped out, the possum had slipped down the stairs and was headed underneath our van. All I saw was its big, furry, waddling rear end. It was as big as a medium-small dog. Thanks for dropping by, possum. I wish you well. Scuttle away now to a place of safety.

3

There is a big, empty room at my parents' house where I grew up. It's so empty it feels heavy, filled only with memory, childhood hopes that fizzled, and youthful dreams that took a dive into the depths of nothingness. A clock—the ticking kind—marks off the seconds of time passing, just as time has passed through years of coming and going. But even now, as empty as this room is, as heavy and memory-filled, it feels like a safe place, a sanctuary. Outdoors, the wind whistles and rushes past. The world races by. Here, despite the long gone hopes and the drifting dreams, all is well.

4

Round is a satisfying shape, whole and complete. Spheres, circles, rings—it's as if the full moon has flung little echoes of herself into the world and tucked away small reflections of her shape here and there. Circles show up in the center of flowers, in growth rings in a tree stump, in mushroom tops, in a bird puffed up in cold weather. And in the way a piece of writing circles back to its beginning. Round is a satisfying shape.

5

On the ceiling of my sunroom today, there's a round spot of light as large as a dinner plate. It's the reflection of the birdbath in the bright morning sun. On one side of this spot of light, the shadow of a citronella leaf edges into the circle. What first caught my eye, though, is the wavering movement of lines that cross the circle. Those are the ripples of water in the birdbath. They've become a flow of shadows drifting across this reflected pool of light. They've become today's wonder.

6

I recently heard of a study that shows that when people listen to the same music, podcast, or story at the same time, their heartbeats rise and fall in sync. I wonder if the same thing happens when we're listening to silence—or near silence. I think of times when I was with groups gathered around a fireplace or a campfire. After talk died down, after songs were sung or stories told, everyone settled into a reverie, simply watching the flames and listening to the crackle of the fire. I like to think that our hearts were beating together.

7

A cold front moved through overnight, taking the temperature from a balmy 70 to below freezing. This morning, the backyard neighbors' roof was covered in frost so thick, it looked like snow. Craggy clouds scoot across the sky aloof and unperturbed. I shiver. Maybe winter has really and truly moved in.

8

Someone once said that poetry is an emotional echo. Today, I'm looking for that emotional echo, the poetry in objects, places, people, and whatever happens to happen. My first object is the spring green mug on my desk, which holds random pens and pencils, nail files, two peacock feathers, and a Chinese bookmark. I've never thought of this mug as having an emotional echo, but as I look at it now, I realize that it does. It says "author" on the side—one of my publishers gave it to me. That in itself holds mixed emotions: satisfaction, regret, frustration. The red pens in the mug remind me that I'm an editor. A whole group of pencils were given to me by an artist friend. Along the side of each pencil is an encouragement like *Let your spirit fly. Chase angels. Joy will find you.* The two peacock feathers are from a flower arrangement at my older son's wedding in Hawaii. The Chinese bookmark was a gift from my younger son, who bought it when he lived in New York City. The emotional echoes are pinging every which way right now. This one mug is not one poem; it's many.

9

Many years ago in Texas, I volunteered to supervise on a bus that picked up children and took them to Sunday School. At one house, we picked up three sisters named Star, Starla, and Starlene. One Sunday, the temperatures were below freezing. In every yard where the bus stopped, frost had dusted the dry brown stubble of grass, the scrubby bushes, and small, bare trees. Everything looked dingy and tired. Until we reached the house of Star, Starla, and Starlene. My jaw dropped, and everyone in the bus leaned into the windows to see. Their bushes and trees were coated with ice and icicles—real ones—of every color in the rainbow. They had been busy having fun with paint and the watering hose. They taught me that sometimes we make our own wonders.

10

A good listener is not only popular everywhere,
But after a while he knows something.

– Wilson Mizner –

After listening to the various voices of the wind—from a whispering breeze to a wailing gale—we know something. After listening to birds—from happy chirps and trills to sharp, loud warning cries—we know something. After listening to dogs—from nips and yips to barks and growls—we know something. Yes. After a while, we know something.

11

Now that the leaves have fallen, nests are visible high in the trees. I'm watching one that's settled among a tangle of branches near the top of an oak. It's rocking in the wind. Last night we had strong winds and tornado warnings and heavy rain with the threat of hail. But there the nest is, still intact, open to the clouded sky. It must be well-woven and securely cradled in the crook where it rests. It's a wonder it hasn't blown down. Of course, it may yet fall before spring. I'm just glad it's still there. I'm glad I can see it.

12

Tonight, I'm sky-watching. Two planets are supposed to form a line with the moon. It starts at twilight when Venus shows up low in the west, bright as usual. She's the brightest light in the heavens except for the moon and is called the morning star when she appears in the sky before dawn and the evening star when she appears after sunset. As I watch, the skies grow darker, and Saturn appears, higher and more toward the south. Pluto is out there near Venus somewhere but is too far away to be visible. (Besides, as my kindergarten grandson reminds me, it's not even a planet!) Over a few minutes, both Venus and Saturn move, and I have to shift to see them between tree branches. Then the moon eases into the picture, waxing a bit past half. This bright white boat sails the skies and soon lines up with those smaller ships that look so close but are so, so far away and make me feel so, so small.

13

The morning sun is melting the frost on roofs and lawns except where there are shadows. So instead of the shadows being dark, they're frosty white. The trunk of one of our elm trees is casting a shadow on the next-door garage roof. Its shadow is a long, rectangular streak of white frost on dark gray shingles. It seems backward for a shadow to be white. But then, nature always has something new up her sleeve, and I always have something to learn.

14

Tonight we have a "Paramount" sky. I call it that, because it reminds me of the ceiling of the Paramount Theater in the town where I grew up. I was quite young when I first saw a movie there, and it's interesting to me that I don't remember what movie I saw. But I remember that the balcony looked like the walls of a castle curving around the sides of the theater toward towers that I think were tops of stairwells. Overhead, pinpoint lights twinkled in the ceiling-sky, and thin clouds drifted across. The clouds were probably made by lights, but I didn't know that.

I was mesmerized. Tonight, real moonlit islands of clouds drift overhead, glowing white against the starry sky, a "Paramount" sky.

15

I'm studying a tri-colored corner opposite from where I'm sitting in my sunroom (which is actually a moon room right now, because it's night). The angled ceiling meets two corners there, and all three planes—the ceiling and both walls—appear to be different colors even though they're all painted an eggshell white. It's a trick of the light from a combination of lamplight in this room, ceiling light drifting in from the kitchen, and reflections of all these lights bouncing off three walls of double-paned windows. All this light from all these angles are making one wall look pale blue-gray, the other wall look white with a hint of peach, and the ceiling look gray-brown. Three different colors meet together at the top point of the corner like the leaves of a shamrock or the blades of a fan. Or like the architectural wonder that they are.

16

The wind is gusty today, making branches sway and dance. The pines, like old-fashioned ladies are fanning the fading azaleas and leafless dogwoods below. And the birds! They're flitting and fluttering among bare branches and creating an exuberant symphony of low calls and high chirps and melodic warbles mid-range. A flock sweeps by high above, sped by tailwinds. It's a dancing, singing, flocking day.

17

How is it that a 60-degree December day has a chill feel, while a 60-degree day in April has a warm feel? Maybe it's psychological in anticipation of where the season is headed weather-wise. Or maybe it's the breeze. Maybe in December, the breeze carries a hint of the cold to come, while April's breeze holds a balmy hint of spring. All I know for sure is that on this 60-degree day, I'm wearing a warm sweater.

18

Low, pale gray clouds sail like ships across a sea of sky this warm, rainy morning. My trees to the west—they're the neighbors' but I think of them as mine because they're framed by my back window and I keep up with how they're doing each day—they're leafless now, of course, so their branches form a clear lace pattern against the sky. It looks like they're sprouting leaf buds. I can see tiny bumps along their twigs. It's possible, I guess. The weather has been unseasonably warm lately. But surely they won't leaf out. Not now. It's either far too early or far too late. But wish me luck telling that to the tree.

19

Smoke is rising from my back neighbors' chimney in lazy plumes. It's slow to disperse against a pale apricot sunrise that fades to white-yellow. Straight overhead, the sky is blue, streaked with vapor trails and feathered winter clouds. I wonder if the neighbors' smoke will rise that high. I wonder if those feathered winter clouds are made of smoke from other chimneys. I wonder if our neighbors' smoke will join them as they drift away.

20

When the vine stops vining
and the hydrangea leaves droop
like disappointed dancers,
when the windflowers drop to the ground
and the creeping Jenny is a tumble of brown,
when the dogwood becomes a bony sculpture,
all elbows and skinny arms and twiggy fingers,
and even the violas bow their happy heads
to the frost,
when the tips of the crape myrtle
are hung with sleeping pods
and the peppers shrivel and go to seed,
then,
only then

the nandina blooms with bright red berries.
Then,
only then
does she take her turn.

– kh –

21

If you were a bird, and lived on high,
You'd lean on the wind when the wind came by,
You'd say to the wind when it took you away:
"That's where I wanted to go today!"

– A. A. Milne –

Winter has only begun, and already I'm looking forward to spring. I'm grateful that the weather foreshadows spring every time winter warms a bit. I'm grateful for the supermarket where year-round I can find the taste of spring in the produce section (ah, blueberries!) and where I can stroll through a garden of fresh flowers in the floral section (Gerbera daisies! Roses! Lilies!). I'm grateful for the feeling of eternal hope and possibility that returns with childhood poems. Autumn leads to winter, but winter leads to spring. And that's where I want to go.

22

Days and months are travelers
of eternity. So are the years
that pass by.

– Matsuo Basho, translated by Nobuyuki Yuasa –

Change changes us. Some of those changes we choose. Others are not our choice. Just look in the mirror. As a sixteenth-century proverb says, "Times change and we with time." The question, then, is not whether to change but how.

23

A blanket of soft, silver-gray clouds
covers the morning sky
as far as I can see.
Even indoors, I feel the weight of it.
I try not to see it as gloomy
but as a protective roof
over the pines and the bare elms.
All is still and quiet.
The whole world seems to have taken a day off.
Rest, the clouds say.
Rest after this busy, crazy year.
Rest under this silver gray blanket of sky.

– kh –

24

My fresh flowers come from the supermarket now. I typically go for mums or carnations, because they seem to last longer than most other flowers. But this week, I was feeling adventurous and bought a mixed bouquet. It did have one salmon-pink carnation as well as mums, the single kind, in white and yellow. But the most interesting blooms were the unfamiliar, pure white, cup-shaped flowers that peeked out here and there among the mums. They were narrow and only a bit longer than my little finger. When I got home, I looked them up in my flower encyclopedia and discovered that they're peach-leaved bellflowers or campanula. Sometimes, that's all the adventure I need for a day.

25

Joy was my grandmother's house—
playing in her den,
staying up late,
eating chocolate ice cream.
Joy was Christmas morning
and sparkly presents,
getting a mosaic set
and arranging the tiles
with real, gray, cement-looking glue.

Joy was getting muddy in pottery class
and not changing clothes until I got home
splattered with mud.
Joy was Friday night,
making a hot fudge sundae
with toasted almonds on top
and eating it slowly.
Joy settled soft inside me,
a deep and private thing.

– kh –

26

Sit in reverie and watch the changing color
of the waves that break
upon the idle seashore of the mind.

– Henry Wadsworth Longfellow –

In my memory, I stand on the shore of the Pacific
Ocean, watching a storm approach in a gray sheet of
rain on the horizon. The wind blows my hair.
Incoming waves crash, and I feel their spray. Then the
surge ebbs, and the water softens into a surf of thin
bubbles washing the shore. The sea holds such
power. I'm both awed and afraid of it. I know I'm right
to respect its rush and roar. Yet, here the sea is,

performing its ebbing, flowing dance for me. And I am grateful. As I leave, I promise I'll come to the sea again someday. From my home far from the sea, I will sit in reverie, and the sea's waves will break upon the idle seashore of my mind. It will be a comfort and a wonder.

27

Serenity means utter calm.
So says the dicionary.
I think of serenity as floating,
totally giving my weight
to water or air or my mattress,
or whatever is holding me up.
Serenity steps back,
away from the buzzing swarm of worries.
Serenity rests,
for as Julian of Norwich said,
"all shall be well,
and all shall be well,
and all manner of things shall be well."

– kh –

28

There's a fun swirly pattern that happens when you beat eggs or whip cream or stir batter or pudding. It's the trail that follows the spoon. You can get creative and make figure eights or wide circles or even a vortex. Shh. Don't tell. This fun is only for cooks.

29

I bought my young grandson a handheld fan with soft blades that don't hurt if you touch them. We were both fascinated as we watched the fan blades turn so fast that they became a blur, and I said that some things go so fast, you can't see them at all. I began to think of all that's invisible in our world: packets of internet information zipping all around us from emails and social media posts. Radio waves. Sound waves. And the wind. So much energy is invisible. Maybe hate and love are forms of energy too. Maybe they're zipping all around us, sent out from our thoughts and dreams and intentions. Maybe it's up to us to flood the world with waves of peace and love.

30

"If you could only sense how important you are to the lives of those you meet; how important you can be to the people you may never even dream of. There is something of yourself that you leave at every meeting with another person." – Fred Rogers

You are a wonder.
Your life is a journey,
and you are the journal,
the diary of life seen through your eyes,
penned by your hand.
You are a poem.
You are a symphony.
You are a tree
changing through the seasons.
You are the path someone follows.
You are the footsteps.
You are a freshet, a river, an ocean.
You are tidal.
You are a story, an epic adventure.
You are a building, a shelter, an archive.
You are a garden,
a sculpture,
a masterpiece,
a drama,
a comedy,
a hope,
a treasure.
You are a miracle,
the grandest of magic.

– kh –

31

And here, at the end, is my wish for you.

I wish you
Love, the soul in full bloom.
Joy, the soul's laughter.
Peace, the calm hum of the soul.
Patience, the soft breath of the soul.
Kindness, the soul's outstretched hand.
Goodness, the soul's high road.
Balance, the soul, centered.
Faithfulness, the steady stance of the soul.
Self-control, the soul's mirror.
Grace, the soul's gift.
Mercy, the soul set free.
Beauty, the delight of the soul.
Wisdom, the soul's treasure chest.
Gratitude, the hearth fire of the soul.
Generosity, the soul's open arms.
Hope, the high window of the soul.
Courage, the soul, face forward.
Creativity, the soul's dance.
Confidence, the soul settled.
Endurance, the second wind of the soul.
Respect, the soul's bow.
Insight, the soul's candle in the dark.
Vision, the soul's mountaintop view.

– kh –